The Overcomers' Anthology: Volume Two

Overcoming Fear

Dr. De'Andrea Matthews, Dr. Mary K. Clark,
Abigail Shade, Aisha Dennis, Angelita Byrd,
Anita F. Morgan, Brian A. Matthews,
Denise Crumbey, Marquita Greene
and Tatrice M. Starks

Claire Aldin Publications
P. O. Box 453
Southfield, MI 48037

ISBN 978-1-7347469-5-2 (paperback)

Printed in the United States of America

Dedication

This anthology is dedicated to anyone who has struggled with any type of fear. Fear comes in all shapes and sizes. Know that you are not alone. May you find comfort and solace as you read the testimonies of these overcomers.

Table of Contents

Overcoming Unspoken Fears

By Dr. De'Andrea Matthews

"Your mother is missing."

"What do you mean missing?!" I practically screamed in the phone. "Where did you leave her? Where did you see her last? How long ago was that?"

The litany of questions continued to spew forth like rising flood waters as my vehicle steadily accelerated through midday traffic, careening through cars like they were standing still. When the call ended, I was just as confused as when it started. My father, who had been caring for my mother since she returned home following a stroke, didn't know where she was. He left her in his brother's apartment while he went to handle some business.

The past four months had been chaotic to say the least. First, my sister and I made an executive decision to no longer allow our mother to drive. Driving behind her was like watching paint dry. Riding in the car with her, felt like the other drivers were in a NASCAR race while we were moving in slow motion. Nope, no more driving. Within weeks after making that decision, mom had her second stroke. The previous stroke had been ten years prior, from which she completely recovered. This time, she was having insurmountable difficulties.

Following a couple weeks stay in the hospital, she needed physical rehabilitation. When she left rehab, she came to stay with me for a couple weeks while the boiler was replaced at their house, which is why my dad was at his brother's apartment instead of at home. On my way to her last known location, the troops had been called in – my sister, my nephew, my uncle, and other concerned parties were all canvasing the city in search of a five-foot seven-inch, dark-skinned, African American woman with short grey hair. I drove past the family home and in the direction that I thought she may have traveled if she were walking. When I met up with my dad and others, there was still no sign of her. The police arrived at the same time as me; while they recounted with my dad the last known whereabouts of my mom, I hit the streets again. This time, I started from her last known location and went towards home.

She insisted that we take her home the entire time she was recuperating. Trying to explain to her homesick soul why it wasn't possible for her to go home when the heat was still out and it was February in Michigan wasn't making any sense to her. I looped back around twice having gone two different routes towards their home before I gave it another shot down a familiar, but not often taken path. Low and behold, I see a purple mid-length coat ahead in the distance. I whipped the car up on the wrong side of the street and hopped out, calling her name. My nose flared as I rustled her into the car. I was infuriated with the small talk she was making, like she didn't just scare us out of our wits. It was a casual conversation with mom, oblivious to the chaos surrounding her disappearance. While driving back to the apartment building, the cops and the worried relatives were all notified that she had been found. Both mom and dad got a good "talking to" that day. Dad couldn't seem to comprehend that his loving wife of over forty years was not the quick-witted, independent, "I can do anything" woman he once knew. She could not be left alone but needed to be monitored twenty-four-seven. Mom still didn't understand why she couldn't go home, which is why she was walking in that direction since no one would take her there.

That fateful day in February was only the beginning of a new type of fear for me. I do not fear losing my parents because I understand that as a part of the circle of life; I will bury them one day. This fear had to do with an aspect of aging that I had not been introduced to or even considered when it came to my parents...and that was them being incapacitated.

Throughout the remainder of that year, I watched as my once vibrant parents – muscle-bound dad and always on the go mom – became people who I barely recognized. I was a bystander, watching as my father who insisted on being a strong husband for his wife became physically weaker himself from Parkinson's. Mom's memory continued to fail, and it was evident that she was suffering from dementia, just like her father had.

The nightmare continued as my father's health declined, ultimately causing him to have a car accident on the expressway. Fortunately, no one was injured, but he recognized that he could have been the cause of someone else's demise, which was enough to keep him off the streets…temporarily. The somberness of the moment was surreal as I sat in the emergency room with him on multiple occasions as the summer months drew to a close. As fall turned into winter, the decline in his health continued, and then one day, I got another phone call.

"Daddy fell, and mom will not open the door!"

My oh so suave sister had panic in her voice. The twenty-five minute drive from my house to theirs only took seventeen minutes. I made it to the front steps in time to see the paramedics carrying my frail father out to the awaiting ambulance wearing nothing more than a bathrobe and socks. His face was swollen and disfigured resembling Will Smith's during the pharmacy scene in *Hitch*. No one still knows how long he was lying on that floor, and mom could not verbalize the answers that my sister and I really needed. Left to put the clues together for ourselves, we calculated the sequence of events that made the most sense. Either way, their beloved home is no longer safe for the two of them. The fall risks are too great, the needed repairs are too expensive, and the type of care they now need requires different living arrangements.

While the saga continues, my prayer is that you never experience the type of fear that moved in like a F4 tornado on that February day. My advice is that regardless of the type of fear you may experience, do not hesitate to reach out to your support circle and please don't go it alone. This chapter is dedicated to my own support network, who knows exactly who they are, and for every child who has ever worn the cape of caregiver. You are the true superheroes.

About the Author

Dr. De'Andrea Matthews is the founder and CEO of Claire Aldin Publications, an award-winning hybrid publishing company, where she transforms manuscripts into literary masterpieces. An entrepreneur, international speaker and author, Dr. Matthews has graced the stages of universities and conferences around the globe, sharing the message that *your adversity can become your greatest strength*. Along with being a member of the Nonfiction Authors Association and The Authors Guild, Dr. Matthews is a recipient of the Diversity Business Leader Award from *Corp! Magazine* and has also received the Top 100 Leaders in Education Award from the Global Forum for Education and Learning (GFEL).

Overcoming the Fear of Relationships

By Marquita Greene

For as long as I can remember, I was always afraid of something. Thankfully, I conquered those childhood fears right before I hit adolescence. I feared not fitting in with those I was around, so I pretended to be petrified of them. Doing so gave me the opportunity to trick or finesse my way into 'fakeships', better known to most as relationships. Being fearful, or pretending to be fearful, made it easier for me to hide my biggest trepidation of all — the fear of being in the foster care system and being a statistic.

With that being said, over the years, I developed a mindset of "leave others be and take care of me." Due to this mindset, most people thought I was selfish, but in reality, that's just the way I have grown to protect myself from others. Being only thirty-five years young, I can attest to various methods that you can use to advance in a productive manner when being confronted with your truth. Taking these steps can be hard; however, they are necessary in order to move forward in life. Let's start from the beginning.

I was lonely and was not okay with being alone. Sometimes, you see things through broken glass and it's easier to focus on the pieces. However, the piece that I chose to focus on was *him*. I put everything else aside and focused on him. Whatever he needed, his happiness, his contentment and whether he wanted me — all of these things mattered most to me. I believe that at one point these feelings were reciprocated. Nevertheless, allow me to share a bit about our relationship.

Normally, I am so wrapped up in myself that I do not focus on the next person. Everything and everyone else becomes secondary to me; but when someone gets my attention, trust, I am all in. And in this instance he just happened to be that beautiful distraction for me.

We spent every possible moment together and it was always so much fun. *How long could this last?* I thought. I felt wonderful when I was with him. Being with him motivated me to do better, to be better and to treat others better. He was the yin to my yang, the moon to my sun and everything that I could possibly want in a mate. We clicked so well; when we were together, nothing else mattered. Then, it was time to cross the line. Once crossed, it came down to the question of whether we would be better or worse.

It happened one night. I was lying in bed while he was getting loaded at some party. I wanted him to come home drunk so he *could not* say no. When he came home, he was hungry, so I made tacos. I wanted him to be satiated and inebriated. I sat while he ate until he was content. After he was done, he got up to leave. As I was making my way to the door, he walked so close that I could feel his breath on my skin.

"Excuse me," he said as he reached around me to open the door. I punched him and said, "I don't bite unless you want me to." The look he gave me said that he wanted to do just that. However, he glanced away and started to open the door.

"I will be right back," he said.

"I want my lick back," I said, trying to edge him on. However, he walked away. Moments later, he sent me a text message.

Well, what's up then? Meet me outside.

I changed into something more "accessible." He came back in and we tussled a little. Then, he sat down and pulled me closer to him. I couldn't believe what happened that night, since he and I had been talking about it for months.

I felt good and liberated; however, I knew that this would change the dynamics of our relationship. I knew he loved me, but I didn't know what to expect going forward. We went to bed that night. Morning came, and it was a new day. We acted like nothing was different, and I liked that.

At first, I thought he would become distant. To my surprise, we started spending more time together. Whenever I needed him, he was there. Things were going too good, and eventually, I became bored. However, I had this fear that something would go wrong and that it would be my fault; and I was right.

One day, while we were relaxing, I decided to start an argument.

"Why didn't you put gas in the car?" I asked. He kept playing his game as if I hadn't said anything. Lifting my foot, I nudged him in his back.

"How come you didn't put gas in the car?" I asked again.

He responded with a chuckle. "You have not been out to the car. How do you know what I did or did not do?"

I replied to him, "You never put gas in the car; that is how I know that you didn't. It is always on me to fill up the car!"

He responded by saying, "Okay, I will take the car to the gas station after this game".

At this point, I'm pretending to be livid so I asked, "Why do I have to wait for your game to be over?" I screamed, throwing the pillow across the room. He paused his game and jumped up, asking me what my problem was. Inwardly, I knew what it was. I was so used to having conflict in my relationships that this situation was just too calm for me. Besides that, nothing felt better than make-up sex. Choke me out, body slam me, pull my hair and insult me. As he went to get gas, I tried to find another thing to argue with him about.

It was not until this relationship ended that I vividly realized my problem. I craved *toxicity* because I feared *intimacy*, which was a result of all the toxic situations that were forced upon me in my youth that had never been dealt with.

Looking back, I think my desire for toxicity stemmed from being raped repeatedly as a child, then again as a teenager which resulted in pregnancy. I lost my virginity to my stepfather. (My stepfather is not my son's father; that was a separate incident.) Therefore, I grew up thinking that I would need to either have hidden relationships or ones that involved rough, degrading sex.

The first time I remember being violated sexually, I knew it was wrong because I hid in the closet afterwards. While hiding, all I could think about was my daddy and wondered *When is my daddy coming back to save me? How come he was not there to prevent this from happening?* With the second violent act, I do not recall how old I was; I just know that I was afraid to go to the bathroom after that because that's how he got to me. I asked myself how come I did not hold my pee? Had I done that, I never would have been violated by my stepbrother. So, at an early age, I had two people who were supposed to protect and love me to sexually abuse me...both my stepfather and my stepbrother.

I did not understand what my stepbrother was doing to me as he forced himself on me. Afterwards, he told me that I better not tell because he would kill me, plus I would get in trouble. In those moments, I knew that I had been victimized and my fear was in the process of becoming a reality. My brothers and I were placed in the foster care system.

In my mind, I was relieved to some extent and felt that we would be in a safe haven with my grandmother's sister. (At least I thought we would be safe.) To my dismay, the atmosphere that I witnessed as a child was nowhere near the reality that I was on the path to endure. The loving married Christian family that I had seen through my innocent eyes was a smoke screen. The things that took place within that home were devastating and just down-right nasty. The other foster kids, including my brothers and me plus two additional cousins all played "house." When it was a person's turn to play the parent, they had to do "parent" things, like kiss or even try to have sex with one another. Due to my past, I thought this was normal, but my conscious wouldn't let me rest. To avoid these activities, I would try to fall asleep before everyone else or read a book in hopes to escape to another world just so that my mind would be at ease with a sense of normalcy.

While there, the most frightening experience I endured was encountering my aunt's husband. One day, I had to go back upstairs to get something I forgot. He trapped me coming down the stairs and stuck his tongue in my mouth. That was the nastiest taste I've ever experienced and one that I will *never* forget. In comparison, I can sit back and remember eating dirt as a kid, but not even that taste was as bad as that encounter.

Thinking back on these things and having enough courage to put pen to paper is a lot for me now. Though a challenge, it was a major breakthrough. These instances not only made me dig deeper, but it also made me decompartmentalize the things that I had suppressed inside in order to make it from day to day. It made me dig deep enough to the point of journaling my nightmares in hope that I would gain headway into an understanding of it all. Even in therapy, we never talked about the things that took place in the home during any of our sessions. They remained secrets. Writing this chapter is my first time disclosing my shame, hurt and fears to anyone aside from select family members.

In reality, I think that these experiences made me reclusive from others. I was afraid of the dark and afraid of going to the restroom. These things literally haunted me. I was unable to shower at other people's homes whenever I spent the night or visited because I thought something horrific would happen to me when I least expected it. If others were present, I would just keep the funk on me until I was back home or until everyone was asleep. I felt safe whenever I was completely alone.

For most of my life, I did not like anyone in my personal space. I feared being touched, whether it was a tap or a hug. If someone reached out to touch or embrace me, my stomach would literally ball up in knots and I would immediately recoil. In fact, I purposely arrived at church late and left church early to avoid anyone trying to hug me. Hugs felt intrusive, and I hated them unless they were hugs from my children or immediate family. Being raised in church, it was customary to give hugs and I did so involuntarily. I loathed it with every part of my being.

As a youth, I felt like I *had* to hug others. To be quite honest, I stopped attending church because it was like a big "Hug-a-Thon," even with COVID-19 going around. Hugging the pastor and first lady were not a problem; it was the congregants who made me shudder. I always wondered the purpose behind touching others. How come everyone seemed to enjoy doing this? It took me a while to understand that these feelings were related to the various traumatic incidents I experienced while growing up.

A few years ago, I decided to work exclusively on myself. I made a list of things I needed to address that were never shared with others. I addressed these issues and dealt with them privately. Through a lot of prayer and meditation, not only did I overcome the things that haunted me as a child, but even the things that I still feared as an adult. I started to develop real healthy relationships as well as trust people again. I have been able to interact with others in a free, loving way that causes no issues on my end. Now, I can hug freely and enjoy being my true self. Since I can now do the things that once taunted me, like embrace others, have fruitful relationships and interactions, I know that I am healed.

Sometimes, I still find myself reflecting on my past and wonder if my life would have been different had I not experienced those traumatic events. I can now honestly and wholeheartedly state that I have overcome the fears and issues that were stunting my growth. I now know that these steps of getting over these obstacles were necessary in developing beneficial relationships with not only friends and family, but more so with my children who are now young adults living their own lives.

It took me a long time to understand that I was only a child and did nothing wrong. In essence, I was a victim of my own environment. After multiple encounters with toxic relationships and years of therapy, I have come to realize that they were the perpetrators and I was the innocent one in the entire situation. Looking back, I can say that I am no longer ashamed. Since I'm now able to speak freely about these things, it's easier for me to breathe. It feels like a weight has been lifted off of my chest. I am no longer embarrassed by my past. I have never felt so radiant, so free, or so in love with myself. God has washed away the fear and the stains that remain are the scars left to remind me of where He has brought me from. He has turned this mess into His masterpiece!

About the Author

Born and raised in Detroit, Michigan, Marquita Greene has dreamed of writing a book since middle school. From journaling to penning poetry in her free time, this Texas resident, pharmacy technician aide and mother of two can now add a new title to her resume: First-time author.

Overcoming the Fear of

COVID-19

By Aisha Dennis

Fear is what I describe as the most paralyzing, yet intangible thing known to man. It has the innate ability to cripple you, rob you, and hold you hostage in life. It robs our minds, our wills, and emotions of the ability to operate in the spirit of liberty and freedom given by God. It does not operate alone. It brings with it anxiety to keep you off balance and unprepared for whatever life throws at you.

My name is Aisha Dennis, and I overcame fear in the face of adversity while fighting for my life against COVID-19 this year. As a healthcare worker, I have worked alongside many healthcare professionals serving in various communities for almost 20 years. In that time frame, I have seen many walks of life enter our doors needing care and exit our doors with a second chance at life. Nationwide, the role of healthcare workers and professionals has changed immensely throughout this global pandemic. Although many believe it all started approximately March of 2020, I recall our hospital saw an influx in what were presumed "flu-like" cases in late October through November of 2019. In my opinion, this continued to what we now know as the COVID-19 pandemic.

According to Yale Medicine, it is known as Severe Acute Respiratory Syndrome Coronavirus 2 (2020). Throughout this pandemic, I woke up every day, got ready for work, and prepared myself for what was on the other side of those elevator doors. Win. Lose. Draw. I was going to support my team in whatever capacity to serve our community and save as many lives as possible. Day in, day out, our team would win, lose, or draw — all at once on some days. I would do my best to ensure the safety of myself and others as well as the family I had to go home to; but one day, I was not so lucky. I woke up one morning drenched in sweat with cold chills and body aches. I just hoped it was a common cold or even a simple case of the flu, but deep down inside I kept hoping it was anything but COVID-19!

In my mind, I began speculating, asking myself how I could have gotten it. I have been diligent with hand hygiene, cleaning my workspace, constantly social distancing, etc. I only went to work and home. Also, before there was ever a pandemic of this nature, I had been diligent with hand hygiene and cleaning my workspace constantly because these habits have been a part of my daily routine for years. I'm known as the germaphobe at home and work, so how did this happen? I'm still not sure how, but a nasal swab confirmed my worst fear. I went to an urgent care, took the scenic route around the back of the building, allowed the staff to perform a nasal swab, and I waited on pins and needles for an email to confirm if I had the infamous virus or not. Approximately twenty-four hours later, I received an email notification. There it was confirmed in BOLD RED LETTERS on my lab report as SARS COV-2! Immediately, I was saddened. I shed a few tears because I really had been diligent and thought I had been taking the proper measures for safety and cleanliness.

So now the fight with myself to mentally and physically fight for my life and not let this illness win in the battlefield of my mind was literally beginning. I know the Bible tells us that so a man (or woman) thinks in their heart, it will be — in other words whatever my thoughts are on any situation, then that's what it will be. The thought process will be the deciding factor of my mood, my mindset, and my heart in my prognosis. So you see, our thought process can be very dangerous if we are fearful, frightened, or anxious.

When it came to battling this disease, I have been terrified at times to be honest because I have seen people make great progress and die days later. I decided to be honest and vulnerable with my circle of influence who pray with me and for me because isolation can be a deadly place in a situation like this. You need to be surrounded by positive fighting people who are encouraging and rooting for your success. I know it sounds simple, right? Wrong!

As a healthcare professional, over the years I prided myself on going beyond what's expected and learning more about disease processes, the populations that are the most adversely affected, the true role of medical history versus present-day facts, as well as survival rates. So it was hard to turn off the wealth of knowledge that told me as a hypertensive person, my odds of beating this were less likely than others. Also, I was reminded that obesity and positive family history for stroke and heart issues would make my journey even scarier. I was fearful and talking to God like "this is not happening!" I didn't even ask God why, I simply said, "Help me, Lord!

Day in and day out the fever, chills, restlessness, loss of smell, and loss of appetite was more than enough to drive me crazy. I remember the day I broke down and cried. I had reached the end of my rope with this entire process: constantly taking my temperature, popping another Tylenol, sleeping endlessly, aching, sweating, or tossing and turning as the days progressed, and it became a bit more challenging just to breathe, cough, and just to merely exist. I remember the day I was in a discouraging place, and I had to call someone who had experienced what I was going through and had survived the wins and losses in this situation. I am forever grateful to her because she got me back to a safe place about my situation spiritually and mentally, and from that point, I was able to move forward and gain strength from her. I thank God for her and the positive people who had been praying, supporting and interceding because it is so important.

In my conversations with God, I said *Lord I did everything I knew to do to prevent this from happening. I did my part and I asked you to cover me daily in the things I couldn't foresee, but never did I think you would allow it or even be able to use it to help someone else.* I guess it goes back to my interpretation of Romans 8:28, which is that no experience is ever wasted, that everything serves a purpose — whether we agree with this or not, it's true.

See in my fear and anxiety, God began to stir my mind by speaking and saying: *What if I want to use this? I don't need your permission! I am God! I told you all things (even this) will work for your good. Do you really trust me like you say? If so, then let me be God and you be patient.* I could use my imagination to transport me to think of how Jesus felt when he asked God if this bitter cup could pass him by, but ultimately, he awakened and said not my will, but Your will be done in this matter. I suppose in the likeness of His spirit I told God, "Okay if this is your will, since it's clearly not mine, help me navigate through it!"

After many tears and some reassuring text messages from friends and family, I decided to change my outlook on my situation. How can God get the glory if I'm whining, crying or weakening my stance? I literally had to talk to myself to rile myself up to victory in my heart and in my mind. I remember thinking, Jesus wasn't like this! I've got to do better. I actually need to be a savage woman of faith right now, but how?

There's a passage of scripture in the Bible that says the Kingdom of Heaven suffers violence and the violent take it by force. So, every day I had to make a conscious decision to force myself to focus on the Word of God and what it said about my situation. I began to declare things like the Bible said, so it could be established in the Earth. Why? Because God tells us He's actively watching over His Word to perform it, so whatever I say will not return to me empty, but it will be accomplished in faith and manifest because God is not a man that He should lie. Therefore, I made a conscious choice to abandon fear and speak the Word, anxiously waiting for it to manifest. Every day when I got up, I would say "Thank you Father that I am healed and not sick. I am above only and not beneath and that by Jesus stripes I am healed. Even though I'm walking through what could potentially be the valley of the shadow of death, I will fear no evil for you are with me and all things, not some things, but all things are working for my good because I'm called according to your purpose! Today and every day, I know that I will live, not die and declare what the Lord has done for me."

So what can I say to the sickness, to this plague that has claimed the lives of over a quarter of a million people in the United States alone? I say if God is for me, who can be successful against me? Nothing! No one! Not even COVID-19!

About the Author

Overcoming obstacles has been the central theme of Aisha Dennis' life. From the loss of both parents by age seven, to surviving the foster care system to being a runaway, Aisha Dennis has a story to tell. She did not allow her past, distractions or a lack of motivation to quench her desire to help others. Always giving back, Aisha can be found working at the hospital, being the "thermostat" for whatever floor she works on while meeting the needs of the people, no matter how big or small. Her favorite saying is based on Romans 8:28: *"No experience is ever wasted."* This saying captures the essence of the life of overcomer, Aisha Dennis.

Overcoming the Fear of Failure

By Angelita Byrd

"If only I were successful."

My thought process consisted of grandiose ideas of how my life would be so much easier — *if only I were successful*. That is how I used to think; however, that was a catalyst for disaster. As I look back on fears I needed to overcome, I realized it was not that simple.

My story begins as a teen mom. Feeling alone, pregnant, and on welfare, I was trying to figure out how to survive. I thought life was over for me that dreadful day my high school vice principal in high school sat me down and said:

"Angelita, you're black, you're fourteen and you're pregnant. You will never be anything in life, so you might as well drop out of school."

The whole trajectory of my life changed in an instant. I could have easily believed him, but in that moment, my mindset changed. I had already entertained those same thoughts about myself before they were ever spoken by him. As I reflect on that day, I can imagine my look of disappointment in response to the one who was supposed to help me become who I was destined to be, despite my circumstances. I quickly changed schools and never looked back.

My quest to discover my identity began as I transitioned into my new school. My family is mixed, and I was always the girl with the light eyes and long "good hair." My fair complexion did not matter anymore, now that I was attending an all-black high school. I could definitively say that I was a black woman. As a black woman, I finally felt a sense of belonging and pride about who I was. There was hope for a better outcome for my future. I was surrounded by peers who not only believed in themselves *but they also believed in me*. This set things off for me in a whole new way. How? Remember the words the vice principal spoke over my future about I'm not supposed to be graduating from high school — let alone be accepted into several different colleges of *my* choosing. Look where I am now. No one could have told me that I would achieve this level of success.

Going away to college was my great escape from my past...the past I never wanted to return to. After careful consideration, Indiana University of Pennsylvania (IUP) was the college I chose to attend. Clear across the great state of Pennsylvania, IUP was far enough to escape the memories of what could have been if I had listened to the vice principal. Much to my surprise, college was no walk in the park. Seeing that I was already not the best student, schoolwork was incredibly challenging for me at times.

My freshman year was filled with wonderful new friendships and falling in love. *Someone wanted to love me?* The girl who ran away from home with average grades and had a three-year-old baby awaiting my return. "No way!" I thought to myself.

I developed friendships with my peers from many parts of the country. Most of the students from my hometown were staying in state. I had my "fall-back girl" who I followed to IUP. She and I grew up together on the same block. She was my witness to everything I was desperately trying to run away from. If there was anyone I could count on, it would be her. Little did I know that I would end up bonding with a group of girls who became my sisters and ultimately "aunties" to my baby girl. When my daughter visited with me on campus, my crew would take turns babysitting while we rotated classes. It was the best feeling in the world — to have that level of support and friendships from a group of women I hardly knew. Another success!

Back to falling in love. I met a guy. He was shy, a man of few words. It was simply something about him that I could not shake off. I told all my new friends that I liked him and they teased me every time he passed by us on campus. I remember the day I got the courage to say hello to him. His parents were packing up his things to leave for that semester. The following semester, we became a hot item and a popular couple on campus. I had my crew and he had his. We were a tight-knit pack.

Having a baby and my lack of academic achievement did not matter to him. He loved me and I loved him; he was my best friend. With him in my life, I felt like I could do or be anything. I never knew I could feel that good about myself or a man. Most of my previous experiences with men were no good until we connected. He was my first true love. This was my first personal success love story.

Success has many meanings; yet the fear factor remains the same. The daunting question that runs through most of our minds is, "What if I fail?" What if I fail and all that I'm doing is for nothing? What if I end up with nothing? What if I prove the principal's words to be true?" The outlook on success in your personal life or business adventures will sometimes trap you in this vicious cycle of the analysis of the paralysis. We all want everything to be *just right*. No one wants to face challenges or setbacks. When we witness success, we typically only see the outcome — not the struggles that come with it.

Our passions drive our purpose. It helps us work through the tough times in our journey towards success. Hence, the reason why I shared my college love story. Love is one of the most powerful emotions on earth. It can move mountains and restore faith in ourselves — especially, when things are falling apart. The love I had for my boyfriend in college helped me develop a love for myself and boosted my confidence about my future. This is also why I believe that to acquire success, you must first figure out *who* you are. Failure will not only test your character; it will show you the areas you need to build in order to be successful.

My personal life experiences prepared me for success. I had to overcome self-doubt and the habit of questioning who I am and what I possess. *Was I good enough or smart enough? Was I even worthy enough for success?* Once I made my mind up and shifted my way of thinking, it became a gamechanger. This new outlook boosted my belief in myself and gave me this unshakable faith and courage to move full speed ahead. Everything seemed to become clearer and the visions of my future seemed so much brighter.

The fears began to fade. I became fearless and feared. People who doubted me began to see that they could not get in my way. If they tried, it was not going to be without a fight.

I had to learn how to fight for myself. I no longer allowed others to shame me or tell me who or what I could become. My mind was made up. I was not that 14-year-old helpless, pregnant black girl anymore, sitting before the vice principal who tried to dictate my destiny. Looking back, I had to grow up so quickly and faced many obstacles. I can look her in the mirror and tell her I am super proud of what she's done with her life. She's lost so much but gained it back tenfold. The one thing she never lost was herself. The many times she felt like life was over with no fight left inside to give, she came out swinging and winning again. Never quitting is the one thing she mastered. I love that more than anything else about her.

As I evolved through life's experiences, I wish I could go back and tell my younger self: "You must have intense focus, integrity, written goals, a mission with a purpose and a never-give-up attitude to succeed in life. No one is coming to save you. No one is going to give you anything you are not willing to work for."

When you see someone who's successful and possesses everything you could ever desire, just know that there are many opposing factors behind the nice house, the fancy cars and extravagant lifestyle. These people have a story that many are unaware of and quite frankly are unable to walk a mile in their shoes to obtain their possessions. I had to learn that the hard way. There will be many sacrifices, sleepless nights, blood, sweat and tears as you claw your way up the success ladder. Anything worth having will never come easy. You must work hard until you figure out a way to make things work for you.

The better life gets, the more challenging it becomes. This is another stage of success that many are not ready to face. Trust and loyalty are huge factors in the equation. Many will betray you and look for ways to take you out in order to inherit what you have built. Therefore, as your lifestyle changes, your circle of friends should change. You are no longer hanging out with the people you love—especially if they do not share the same outlook in life. Successful people tend to hang around other successful, like-minded individuals.

Success always comes back full circle to your personal life. It is said that if you hang around four broke friends, you are bound to become the fifth. Likewise, if you hang around four rich friends, you are bound to become the fifth. The fear of losing someone you love over your lifestyle choices is a personal battle you must overcome. I'm not suggesting that you kick your friends completely out of your life. Friends should be as eclectic as your shoe collection. There are some shoes you wear more often than others because they go with everything. That is how it works with your circle of influence while you are building your success story.

There will be friends who support you and others who will think you are crazy out of your mind. Most times, the friends who think you're "crazy," secretly envy you and wish they could do what you do. The only difference between you and them: You did it scared. You embraced ways to overcome fears in the midst of your own battle. Overcoming fear is a constant, inner battle. "Fear nothing but fear itself, the paraphrased quote from Franklin D. Roosevelt, is so much easier said than done. As you overcome, you will have your "A-ha!" moment, realizing that fear will always be a part of your success. Overcoming it is a part of a never-ending process. I'm here to testify that it's all worth it!

"Courage is resistance to fear, mastery of fear, not absence of fear."

~Mark Twain

I am not a quitter; it's not over by a long shot. I've had many great success stories over the years. I'm constantly hungry for more. Now in my late 40's, I feel that the best is yet to come. God has been preparing my success story to inspire many around the world. With plans to transition into a world-renowned speaker/storyteller and bestselling author, I finally feel a strong sense of confidence to open myself up to who I am, and not what others assumed me to be. As I am writing and sharing my thoughts on overcoming my fears of success, a bit of anxiety and fear creeps in at the thought of the next great chapter of my life. Are you ready? I know I am!

As you read my story, we are experiencing death around the globe from a virus that many of us has never heard of. Cities and states all over have been shut down and we have now transitioned into this "new normal" that no one, including myself, want any parts of. However, the interesting twist is that I feel like I was prepared for this madness.

At first, I would feel guilty when others would check in with me to see how I'm doing. I would reply, "I'm doing great; I could not be happier." How can she be so happy when the world is in shambles and people are getting sick and dying? I have been conditioned this way, as you have read through a fraction of my life story of success. Have I had setbacks? Absolutely! Disappointments? Without a doubt! Fears? Duh! A virus is going around that can kill me or anyone I know and love. So, why am I so darn happy?

Happiness is a choice, no matter the circumstances you are facing. Happiness helps you boost your moral. When your moral is high, your energy levels are high; and when your energy is high, you get more things done. In the short explanation of it all, it has everything to do with being *disciplined*. I have not worked a nine-to-five job since 1997. I've hustled and busted my tail and created many opportunities for myself from the comfort of my home. When everyone was in transition of not having to "beat the traffic" to get their jobs, my life and everyday routine didn't change.

I've mentioned how you must be willing to work really hard until you figure out how to make things work for you. I've been fortunate over the years of creating a residual lifestyle that pays me whether I get out of bed or not. While many friends, family and associates laughed at me and said I would never make any money in the direct sales industry, I got the last laugh when I was living life, traveling around the world while they were stuck behind a cubicle. I really do not feel like I'm missing out on much of anything being stuck at home. I have been fortunate over the years to travel to many parts of the world. I'm not wealthy, but I am free. Freedom is priceless to me. That was a huge goal I set and achieved. I wanted and needed to be free.

Dear Mr. Vice Principal,

Thank you for telling me I would never be nothing. You helped me to overcome fears and become something extraordinary. All that pain was turned into power. I have a faith that is unshakable. If only you could see that little black 14-year-old girl today. I think you would be so proud. I will never forget you. You probably don't even remember me. I am so thankful and grateful for our time together. I am certain you didn't know, at that time, those unspeakable words would propel me towards success.

If I can do it, you can too. Overcome your fears and dream big! You got this!

About the Author

Despite negative words spoken over her life, serial entrepreneur Angelita Byrd overcame them all. Persevering through the trials of being a teenage mother to co-authoring two books in the midst of a pandemic, Angelita is determined to live her best life. This mother and grandmother loves to travel the world and shares her message: *If she can overcome, you can, too!*

Overcoming the Fear of Judgment

By Abigail Shade

From the foundation of my very being, I've endured things that no one—much less a child—should suffer. From childhood rape and the feeling of abandonment, to adultery and mental illness, how I've dealt with each of these obstacles truly makes me note that with God, this impossible walk was made possible.

As a child, I pictured marriage as this "road of forever" with no major issues. Perhaps a mere disagreement here or there. You know, the fairy tale with the happy ending that every princess gets the knight in shining armor...the big house on the hill with the little white picket fence, maybe a little dog, "one and a half" kids, and a life with no worries. No one explained to me the amount of work it would take to succeed. No one explained that there would be no sick days, no vacations, no calling in, no time outs, and no saying, "Go home." Life doesn't come with a manual, and I had no role model to emulate.

My father was married with a plethora of kids born outside of his union, and my mother was living a life with a long-term fiancé who was unfaithful to her. Despite his cheating ways, my mother always took him back. My grandmother was a single parent who was estranged from her husband, my grandfather, due to him being an alcoholic. He became a different person while ingesting that liquid courage. He lived in a different state for 21 years. My grandmother was married for 37 years until his demise in 1996. The reality is this: Marriage is a blessing and yes, it takes more than we are taught to make it work. It takes God being first in both parties' lives. It takes a strong prayer life, along with occasional counseling, openness, communication (being silent, listening, and hearing), honesty, understanding, flexibility and compromise. It takes consistency in romance, strong moral foundation, agreement, and most importantly, respect in all aspects of the union.

Loneliness was my constant struggle while growing up. What I failed to see was that loneliness transitioned into fear--even in my marriage, largely due to the feeling of always being placed on the back burner. Everyone and everything came before me and because of the loneliness that I felt during my marriage I always had a "Plan B"—a side dude—in who nine times out of ten, was married himself. We both knew there could be no real expectations of one another simply because we both had families of our own. Boundaries and expectations were set in the beginning, and no further discussion was needed. However, the most vivid relationship is what I called "The Lion's Den."

The Lion's Den was a game changer. In that relationship, I became the second wife in my best friends' marriage with her, her husband and their kids. Keep in mind that I was still married. Our kids played together, we ate together, and we worshipped together. At one point, we even lived together while I left my husband in the house all alone for almost a year. Although I knew that sin was wrong, it felt so good. The soul ties were strong and I couldn't see the entanglement from within. This relationship was my kryptonite. The very thoughts of him and this relationship made me weak. His love for me, his affection, attentiveness, concern, inspiration, motivation, and his forehead kisses not only made me melt, but they also made me forget all about my own marriage and salvation. This thing literally had me bound.

I didn't realize just how deep I was involved until I confessed to my best friend who I call "Sissy." One day when she first visited me at The Lion's Den, as she walked toward the porch upon arrival, she said that she saw the spirits of me and the "lion" from the den smiling, laughing, and playing with each other. At that point, it had no meaning to me earthly or prophetically, mainly because she had no clue what I was involved in. Therefore, I laughed at the comment and kept it moving.

I knew the Word; I knew right from wrong and was aware of the calling on my life. In my mind and heart, I knew that I would be judged and reprimanded for my sins; however, what was most dangerous was the thought of dying in sin and contemplating if my soul would be saved or would I be condemned to an eternal hell. I feared being seen as an adulterer. Would I be forgiven, mainly in the eyes of the Father? Would others view me as being forgiven or as an adulterer? After all, it was hard for me to see *myself* as forgiven; so why should anyone else?

I operated on a relentless cycle of "repent and repeat." I would ask for deliverance, get delivered and go right back into the same sin. I became what I call an "R&R repeat offender." I knew that I had to stop putting myself in the same situations that God had already taken me out of. I was trying to fill a void that couldn't be filled by anyone except the Father Himself. My soul wanted salvation and my flesh wanted more and more of this sin. It was like a big sinkhole sucking me in. This battle within had been surrendered by flesh alone.

James 5:16 says that we are to confess our sins to one another and pray for each other so that we can be healed, for the prayer of a righteous person is powerful and effective. Not only did I fear being judged or being the new gossip topic, but I feared church hurt. Therefore, I kept my promiscuous behavior to myself. However, I didn't realize that some people in the church were secretly dealing with some of the same demons that I was battling with.

Finally, one day over a year into this lust-filled situation, I sat down and I cried out to God. I repented and I prayed to God, telling Him that I was struggling. This reoccurring demon was riding me, and I could no longer deal with this thing alone. I needed help and real deliverance. I needed someone to help me fight in this combat zone, someone to hold me accountable. Despite my fear of judgment, I had to talk to someone because the battle within was real. I felt condemned. I confessed to my spiritual sister all that I had done, all that I was feeling, and all that I was going through. Before I knew it, within this conversation, without me asking, she began holding me accountable and walking with me. God was answering my prayers and using her whether she knew it or not.

Though I was never caught in the act like the unnamed woman in John 8:3-11, my husband wasn't stupid. Although he may not have known details, I'm adamant that he had an idea of what was going on. I watched his heart break while I was in sin. I repented, ended the relationship with "The Lion's Den" and moved myself and the kids back home. This was a struggle because the bondage from the soul ties were strong. The love and compassion that I carried for him were deeper than anything that I had ever endured before. I hadn't even felt this deep for my own husband — well, not in years.

It took lots of prayer and me making multiple pacts with my "Sissy" to keep me grounded, focused and from backsliding. I told her that whenever I had those thoughts, I would need to call her to pray, cry, scream and whatever else it would take to keep me steadfast on this path. I had asked for forgiveness so many times, but repeated the same sin I had repented for. I feared that at some point, my grace was running out and forgiveness would be no more.

The thought of God's grace, mercy, and forgiveness coming to a halt was petrifying. Biblically, the punishment for adultery surely was death, and that sent me into a panic. My ultimate fear became whether I was going to live or die with a side of questioning if my death would be spiritual, natural, or both. I began to panic because I had kids to care for and I didn't know what would happen to them.

I still had yet to understand that one could heal from a toxic relationship over time with a multitude of prayer and support, even if that outcome meant having no relationship with said individuals. However, if you don't heal *that thang* (and yes, I said *that thang*) that attracted you to them or the situation, you will meet again. Same demon, just in a different host (familiar spirits). Some of yawl not gone catch that!

It took about two years before I became stable and realigned myself under the umbrella of God within my marriage. Within this timeframe, my husband and I decided that relocation was best for us and our family. Little did I know that tests and trials would come with this obedience. The kids and I attempted to relocate in 2016, but returned home in a matter of months after our living arrangements with family didn't work out as planned. That following year, we attempted to relocate again. We moved with nothing except the clothes in our suitcases. We had no vehicle; we had to solely depend on others in a place with no public transportation. It was hard to grasp that my husband and I had to be separated in order to obtain residence by that state's law for housing, especially seeing that we were just starting all over again.

We agreed that he would stay in our home state and I would stay with the kids and family. We did this to gain full-time employment and establish residency in the state in hopes of buying a home to start anew. Since I was in the medical field, it was easier for me to obtain employment. I sought employment and gained stability for the things needed for our fresh start. However, during this process of working, dealing with kids alone and the time difference played a drastic role in what I was feeling.

During this year of separation, that feeling of loneliness came back to visit; however, it didn't come alone. This time, it brought friends back with it—the fear of regret, deception, hatred, depression, lying, and uneasiness because there was lack of control, and fear of the unknown. Six months had passed before I met this guy, who was a friend of the relatives I was staying with. I found a male friend who slowly began to fill those voids.

In the beginning, we were just friends. Over time, he began doing the simple things that I felt my husband should've been doing, even in his absence. He made sure that I was able to get to and from work. He made sure the kids were okay and had dinner or breakfast on the days I had to work. Frequently, I worked double shifts because I had to send funds home to help with the house there, along with paying my way here while we made pallets on someone else's floor. I had a man present, in the flesh, being attentive and in my ear telling me it's something about you that I can't put my finger on that draws me to you. My response was, "it's my anointing." Then, of course, sex came into play, and my fear became reality again. I was back in the same sin again.

My husband knew that this gentleman had a presence in my life because I promised God and myself after "The Lion's Den" that there will be no more secrets. Of course, he was suspicious despite me assuring him that nothing was going on. He feared losing me as I had already felt that I had lost him months after relocation. The arguments between us became frequent. Quite often, I would tell him, "I'm married, but yet I'm lonely and feeling like a single parent." Despite the fact that I knew that *we* decided to make this move together after consulting God through fasting and prayer, it didn't matter. Adultery engulfed me again.

I got sick during a road trip with my family. My illness called for an emergency surgery the day after Christmas. On the day of surgery, my male friend was there with me; my family had to work and my immediate family resided in my hometown. After the surgery, I temporarily moved in with him because he had a bed. During the healing process, I could no longer get up and down from a pallet nor a blow-up mattress. My friend was the one taking care of me in sickness and in health while my husband, who resided in another state, was calling our daughter to get updates on me as I was being rushed back for post-surgical complications. After recovery, I went back to stay with the family; however, my conversations with my husband grew shorter and my anger toward him grew into rage. I felt that he didn't care or love me anymore. He just let a total stranger take care of his wife and kids *knowingly* without an attempt to surface.

As time went on, my husband finally came to visit for my birthday and my daughter's birthday, which are a day apart from each other. I offered to introduce him to the guy who was helping us out, and he refused.

"Why would I want to meet the man that is my replacement?" my husband asked.

I spent every day that I was not working with my husband. When I was working, he dropped me off and picked me up. The day he left to go home, we looked at houses, made a choice and decided to move forward in the purchasing process. I had a whole breakdown because I didn't want him to leave me here. I burst into tears, begging for him not to leave us here alone anymore. I told him we needed him and how much I missed him and us. I could see the tears forming in his eyes.

"We just made an offer on that house, it won't be long before I'm here," my husband said. "I'm not letting you go; you're my wife and I love you. Just let me go back, finish packing the house and I'll be here before you know it. Trust me, I'm coming!"

I didn't know that would be my last time seeing, holding, and touching my husband. Two weeks before his arrival and our closing, he was killed in a car accident.

Life as I knew it had changed again, and this time, it was not by my choice! I feared that because of my wrongdoings, I was being punished. I thought that it was because of my sin that he was no longer here. I was upset with myself because I missed out on the time I could've spent with him and had better conversation choices. I could never get that time back. The time that I spent being angry was all for what? Then the fear of death raised its beastly head and brought depression, regret, and many other friends. Grief brings about a multitude of things and there is no time frame for it to happen. I learned it looks and feels differently for everyone.

After a rough first year following his demise, I attempted to return to work, bought a house and a car. I put all of us in counseling and attempted to have a life with abundance. However, my emotions were not ready. In talking to my mother-in-law and her coming to visit, I began to wonder exactly what did my husband mean when he asked why would he want to meet his replacement? After hearing and listening to her tell me that I am still young and have a whole life ahead of me, I was unsure of what to do or feel. So after being married for almost 20 years, I was fearful of dating. New people, the unknown, getting to know different people is not my thing. So I attempted a relationship with the only guy that I knew here. I learned that we were better as friends; however, some benefits stayed in place.

In 2020, during this pandemic, I lost my mother-in-law. I became highly paranoid that my demise was next. There was a picture of my husband, my mother-in law, myself, and her two brothers on the nightstand next to my bed. My husband died two weeks after his uncle, and his mother died two weeks after her last living brother in that picture. Out of everyone pictured, I am the only one left living. I felt like I was literally losing my mind. I felt like people were going to think that I was crazy, so I secluded myself from my kids, quit answering my phone altogether and went on a fast.

During this fast, I told God all that I was dealing with. I asked for forgiveness, sat quietly and cried a lot, including crying myself to sleep for over two months straight. When I finally heard God talking to me, He said that I had a clean slate and was forgiven for all. I heard Him say that I had to stay clean, and if I didn't quit, I would face death. (This time it wasn't me fearing death; it was God's direct words to me as a warning). I didn't want to find out whether from physical, natural, or both. So, knowing the only sin that I was aware of was fornication, I had a conversation with my partner and explained where I was on this Christian walk. I told him that we could no longer have *any form of sex* in our relationship unless we were to become married. He understood and I have been clean ever since. After God said He would continuously bless me if I walked in my destiny, in boldness, and served Him with a clean spirit that He will be my provider. I couldn't resist the offer that came from the Father.

Now that I have found my way back on this path to this Christian journey, I am motivated and standing on the Word of God and prayer. I have learned that I have to cover myself daily, several times a day, to keep myself full of the Word with no way for the enemy to creep in. I am careful with whom I allow in my space. It was prayer that brought me through, and it is prayer and faith that sustains me. I have to remember His promises while trusting and believing that He is God, and God all by Himself.

We (believers, nonbelievers, men, women, and children) live in a constant fear of judgment from people who we think and feel will not understand the obstacles we've faced. Fearing the judgment of others makes us hide and run from the world. Despite what we understand, note that we are the best and the worst judge of character of ourselves. In reality, it's hard for us to forgive ourselves even after being forgiven. We struggle with letting go of the shame that we carry for the sin(s) that we have committed.

We consistently hide and isolate ourselves for these reasons, not realizing that we are hiding the best parts of ourselves. So, we live as prisoners to self to hide the scars, the tears, and the battle wounds. The Lord says He will forgive it all, so don't judge yourself. Instead learn to be vulnerable, transparent, and embrace your experiences because they're your own. Walk bold in your deliverance. They're the things that set you apart from others. They are the things that uniquely make you *you*. I get that no Christian wants to confess to the church, pastor, brother or sister in Christ for that matter that they're struggling with sexual sin or any other sin. But I've learned that we become prisoners of our past unless we confront it. Never discount the test that gives you the testimony, despite the sin. There is always at least one soul out there who is waiting for you and needs to hear your testimony because they are fighting through it, too.

Throughout this process, I've had to remind myself that fear cripples, silences, and stifles purpose. I learned from experience that a little mustard seed of faith can move mountains! You are not defined by your past, but are chosen by God for greatness. Get it together, let go of the guilt, hurt and shame. You are not out here alone. Many people are struggling with some of the same fears and circumstances. Be transparent; be unapologetically you. Take the good and the bad and find the light in it. Walk boldly, for you have people who are stagnant and waiting on you.

About the Author

Forewarned by God to prepare for what lies ahead, Abigail Shade has been shaped by a myriad of life experiences. Prompted to move her family across country for a fresh start, she learned to depend on the voice of God as her compass. Outside of her twenty years working in the healthcare sector, Abigail's culinary gifts serves as her platform to minister and engage with women from all walks of life. Her ministry evolved into a safe haven for troubled women to embrace freedom through expression of art. Abigail motivates others to express and even redirect anxiety and fear to creating culinary masterpieces. After reconnecting with her divine identity, purpose and gifts, Abigail is grateful to have overcome multiple traumas and the fear associated with it. Empowered to serve, Abigail's mission is to help others triumph over the woes of trauma and fear by planting seeds of hope that will cultivate and flourish with the light of Christ.

Overcoming Fears Around Childhood Rejection

By Denise Crumbey

Fear not, for I am with you; be not dismayed, for I am your God;
I will strengthen you, I will help you, I will uphold you with my
righteous right hand.
-Isaiah 41:10 ESV

It is so easy to be afraid when you don't know who you have on your side. It is also easy to slip into what seems like an endless cycle of repeating experiences for different (but similar) situations in your life. I must tell you it was like that for me in several areas of my life. I was controlled by fear. It walked with me, talked with me, became my thoughts, affected my actions and caused me to question the very fabric of who I was.

How can a four-letter word do so much damage? Well, when you start to believe the lies of it (fear), then the pathway to damage is clear. Though it is a small word, the belief in it is deadly. People kill because of their belief in it. They commit adultery, they manipulate, they hide or avoid because of it, they make excuses because of it, they commit suicide, compromise their morals and so on. You get the gist of what I am implying here.

I was paralyzed by it, afraid that I would fail at anything I tried. I was fearful of what it would look like if I succeeded. I was in a revolving door, too afraid to step out and believe in myself, my gifts, and my talents, too afraid to trust the truths that God had already spoken about me. I was afraid of success and failure at the same time. Fear had crippled my life in so many different areas, but I believe it all originated from one source, and I believe that this is the case for you too. It is my hope this chapter will help you to identify the point of origin where fear began its imprisonment of your life. As you read on, think about what you are fearful of and try to remember where it started—it could save your life. This chapter will change your perspective and bring an ending to the plague and imprisonment of fear.

There are many areas of fear I could talk about, but right now we are going to focus on the fear of rejection. For some of us, this type of fear started before we were born. It started right in the womb, from the very date of our awareness. Often, we are unaware of why we respond to things a certain way, more often than not it is due to some type of experience that traumatized us as kids.

My experience began in the womb. I know, I know—some of you are saying, "the womb, come on!" There is research about infant responses regarding fetal exposure to certain sounds: a mother's heartbeat or voice, a story being read to them repeatedly, etc., and the results were surprising. Several of these studies were able to prove that infants were affected by what they heard in the womb. I'm not going to bombard you with a bunch of science, but I do want you to understand that it is possible that you can experience trauma in one of the safest places: your mother's womb.

As far as I can remember, I dreamed of a life that involved that picture-perfect American family. I imagined my mom and dad together, still married, with me and my sisters. But as I grew older, it became painfully clear that would never happen. Nevertheless, I loved my father and yearned for a movie-worthy father-daughter bond. Of course, it would never happen.

I would find out later in my twenties that my father never believed I was his daughter. It was a painful thing to hear, but then again, it should have never surprised me. You see I always felt that my father treated me differently and rightfully so. You may be wondering what this has to do with a mother's womb and the fear of rejection. It has everything to do with it. My father never thought I was his, and throughout my mother's pregnancy with me, he made sure he voiced his opinion about it.

The Saturday I was born, he never bothered to show at the hospital. You see, that is where the seed of rejection was planted — there in my mother's womb. It (the seed of rejection) was watered shortly after my birth, when my father was a no-show. You see rejection was birthed right along with me. This led to me being a people pleaser because I was scared others would reject me. I was scared of being rejected like my father rejected me. In almost every area of my life, I could see how the fear of rejection was interwoven within me. It stunted my growth, it restricted my creativity, muzzled my voice, and stifled my development, and it all started from the words spoken while I was in the womb and resonated throughout my life.

Maybe you can identify with this. Maybe you can survey your life to see when the seed of fear was planted. I was fortunate that the Holy Spirit revealed my starting point, through painful questions and unwanted answers. I asked my mother if my father came to the hospital after I was born. When I found out he was not there, it confirmed what the Holy Spirit revealed to me. My father had a fear, and he transferred that fear to me, and I had been living with it ever since.

My mother could not protect me from the words that spilled out of his mouth. She could not protect me from his rejection that day and other times throughout my life. She could not protect me from his final rejection and death of our relationship at the age of 40, when my worst fear came true: The words coming from my father that he did not want me or my sisters in his life, the rejection that I had been running from all my life. God held me until I was strong enough to accept his final rejection and face one of my worst fears.

I want to encourage you to survey your life, take a deeper look into your responses and emotions. Ask God to reveal where and when the seed of fear was planted in your life. It may surprise you. Though I was protected in my mother's womb, somehow, my father's words still found a way to penetrate her fortress, inserting the fear of rejection and the start of a source of pain interlaced within my thoughts, materializing through my actions. I gave every ounce of love I could give to my father, and it was not enough. He still rejected me, but God held me when my father knocked me to my knees with his final rejection. Now I understood the source and the trigger.

It wasn't until I realized this that I could identify the source of my struggles and begin to combat it. I was able to see how this fear manifested itself in other areas of my life. I began to see the triggers of rejection (like a break-up with a boyfriend, teasing by kids, rejection of a spouse, etc.) that led to my mental incapacitation. Once you are able to recognize the root of your fear, it will help you to understand your triggers, and bring comprehension to your emotional instability. Your perception will change. By identifying your triggers, you will be able to craft a positive response instead of a negative one through the activation of God's Word.

God's Word? Yes, God's Word! It breathes life and will restore life to the parts of your existence that were dead. Things like the gifts and talents God gave you will be refreshed, and your ability to love again will be restored. You will be able to feel again, to forgive, to release people from the prison you held them in all these years and in doing so, release yourself from your own. God's Word will transform you. He loves you and has never rejected you. Here is a scripture I want you to recite and repeat to yourself every time rejection pops its head up:

For you formed my inward parts;

you knitted me together in my mother's womb.

I praise you, for I am fearfully and wonderfully made.

-Psalm 139:13-14a ESV

You are fearfully and wonderfully made. God loves you. He made you. He loves you so much that you are reading this book. He loved you so much that He provided you with a guide called the Holy Bible to help encourage you through this life. If you are not encouraged, today you can start to do just that – be encouraged. Take this verse, memorize it, and every time you start to feel rejected, remember that God wants you. He will leave ninety-nine sheep to come back for the one that is lost. That means He will come looking for you and will not leave you. Does that sound like someone who doesn't want you? Does that sound like someone who will reject you? Furthermore, when people reject you and who you are, remember that you are fearfully and wonderfully made, remember that God formed you and knitted you together in your mother's womb. You are special to Him. Your birth was not an accident (no matter the circumstance in which you were conceived).

What I need for you to understand is that God had a plan for you before you were born. In the book of Jeremiah, in the first chapter and the fifth verse, the Bible says, "Before I formed you in the womb, I knew you, and before you were born, I consecrated you; I appointed you a prophet to the nations." He was speaking to Jeremiah, but this Word applies to you as well. He knew you before you were born, He anointed you and appointed you for your specific task.

You no longer have to operate in fear; you no longer have to fear rejection. Remember, like the verse at the beginning of this chapter stated: God is with you, do not fear, He will make you strong, He will protect you with His arm and give you victories. He will give you the victory over fear, but you will have to put in the work. He is your God and He has not rejected you. So, let the journey to self-discovery begin. Let's examine the root of our fear and demolish it with the Word of God.

This is to freedom from fear. This is to your empowerment through God's Word. Remove the shackles and start your healing process.

About the Author

Denise Crumbey is an inspirational poet, author and artist. Driven by her call to transform the lives of others, she creates projects that initiate healing and empowerment. A native of Detroit, Michigan, Denise shares her messages on radio shows, at public schools, on college campuses and at churches. She is the director of intercessory prayer at Visions International Ministry, where she worships with her husband, Carl and their seven children.

Overcoming the Web of Fear

By Anita F. Morgan

Like so many others, the majority of my life was lived in fear. Fear of being abandoned, fear of being misunderstood, fear of success, fear of authority and fear of the Lord. Fear, fear, fear.

From the time of my earliest childhood memories — even from age one, I remember many things. I had a keen fear of abandonment. My life was filled with many good times and warm memories; however, the spirit of fear crept in and spun its vicious web in my life. A variety of fears revolved around my life. I never expressed any of these fears to anyone. As an adult, these fears kept me locked in perpetual procrastination, seeking perfection, afraid of others while being extremely defensive and angry. I was so on the defense about everything. I would lash out in anger to those closest to me. I even was afraid of God. Throughout my life, I sought God's approval and love so much that it hindered my ability to develop a close bond with Him. I only sought validation and did not know how to grow closer through His love for me.

The spirit of fear was so strong that I contemplated suicide. Afraid of living life, I felt worthless, stupid, retarded, ugly and rejected. You might think that all these feelings have nothing to do with fear, but fear was the doorway that allowed these spirits to enter my life and control my behavior.

It took many years, including going to seminary, working to become a minister and eventually an elder that I learned to face these spirits, including the most dreadful one of all, the spirit of fear. My biggest asset in these moments was my godly circle of friends. These people taught, encouraged and believed in me when I was unable to do any of that for myself. They did not allow me to continue in destructive thoughts and behaviors. Even with them in my life, the Lord God helped me to understand that none of them could do what truly needed to be done. Even at the height of fear, I was able to overcome, and the light — which is Christ — began to break through that darkness and destroy the web that I felt I had been trapped in my entire life.

I pray most earnestly that through my testimony, you can understand how you, too, overcome fear. It is not easy; it takes a lot of work, courage and boldness to overcome. There will be days filled with tears, and days when you seem to be paralyzed from taking the necessary steps forward. You must step out of your normal pattern of thinking and living, and truly rely on the Word of God to overcome this deceptive spirit. Deliverance may come in a day or in several months. You must work with the Holy Spirit of God to achieve deliverance. Trust when I say that you have not begun to live until you are free from the grasp of fear. It is only through

Jesus Christ that this can happen. There is hope, there is light, there is freedom!

Spinning the Web of Fear

The spirit of fear is likened to a spider waiting to form a web. It forms a web through various circumstances in one's most formative years — even in the womb. Some people grow in nurturing, loving and protective households; unfortunately, for many of us, our lives are the complete opposite. Sadly, fear is formed at the heart of a family. It's done most often through the first authority figures we have — our parents and grandparents, aunts and uncles or even servants of various religions. Satan and his demonic servants use the ones closest to us — majority of the time unbeknownst to them, because family and closest friends tend to be the ones who are directly connected to us and have the most access.

The purpose of this spirit is to paralyze and kill all effectiveness we would have before we realize *who* we are, our purpose and potential. This spirit of fear goes so far as to make us try to destroy ourselves through various means. The spirit of fear is a foundational spirit that builds a platform for other demonic strongholds. It keeps us from forming healthy, productive relationships, especially in our relationship with the Lord. Because this spirit operates through our first authority figures, it directly influences our perception of the Lord and our trust in Him. As a result, we cut ourselves off emotionally and spiritually from Him, which keeps us from receiving the healing, deliverance and salvation that comes through Christ Jesus.

Fear works with other familiar spirits, in conjunction with generational curses and outside demonic influences within your immediate environment.

Trapped in the Web

Fear had me in a place where I was afraid of authority figures — mainly those who were supposed to provide care for me in the absence of my father. I lived in three different homes. In two of those homes, I was mentally and physically abused. I was told that I was not wanted by either my mother or my father. My father sent me to live with these people, instead of my mother. This played a part in my fear of abandonment. When he had custody, he told me that he loved me so much, but that he was old and could not take care of me. He said he would die one day and I would be on my own. For a child of four or five years old, that was frightening. Loving my father the way I did, I was afraid to be left alone, especially not knowing if I would even see my mother again.

In two of the homes, the men of each household were leaders in the church. One was a bishop and the other a pastor. The first place I lived was the bishop's house. We went to church at least four times a week. It was in church where I felt the best because I was able to just be myself. I was allowed to sing in the choir, even though I did not know the words. My father also attended this church, and I had been there with him before living with this couple. I was responsible for helping to light the candles for communion, carrying Bibles and keeping the choir robes in order. I was five years old at that time and loved every bit of it. I loved being in church because in my mind, I felt that God was there and I was protected. That was the only place where I felt safe.

The bishop was kind to me. The wife did not want me to communicate with him, but I would sit with him and watch Kenneth Copeland, and *The 700 Club*, and *Wheel of Fortune*. I used to sit by his bedside as he rested. He would tell me about God when his wife was not around. He was the only one in the house who told my father that I was a good girl, and that I was smart. While living in this home, I learned that no matter what I said, it was going to be misunderstood. Everything I said was twisted, and the fear of God's terrible wrath also came from this house. The wife told me that God would strike me down and that I was going to hell whenever she was mad at me, and for that matter, her own grandchild.

While I was living in this home, that's when I first saw my mother and stepfather (whom to this day I consider as my second father), after almost a year. When my mom's visit was up, I chased her car as she left. I was beaten with an extension cord for chasing her car. I also chased my father's car when he left, too. My only friend in that household was a rottweiler. I was told that this dog was very aggressive, but ironically, this dog lost his life defending me from them. It was a sad day when the pound came and got him to be put down. While living in this household, I saw my first dead body, and was introduced to suicide. My friends who lived next door were brother and sister. Their mother hanged herself in their family garage. When we went in the garage to play, we found her hanging in there. To this day, I can feel the fear of my friends, the fear of losing my own parents, and the terror of death.

That was the last place I lived before I was "rescued" by my mom. Did I ever have good times in that home? At first, yes; but by the end, living there was a nightmare. They made unjust accusations against me to my father. I was accused of stealing $500 from a beauty shop. As a result, I got a beating from my father. Not long after, my father found out from the man who lost his money that I returned it. That man bought me this huge gumball machine—bigger than I was, along with a pretty dress, socks, shoes and underclothes. My father did apologize, but the pastor and his wife kept calling me a thief and told their friends not to trust me.

I was told that I was there because I made a fool out of them and neither one of my parents wanted me. She told me that I was dumb and stupid, and no one wanted me. I was also informed that if they were not friends with my father, they would not want me either. That is when the beating commenced. I was blamed for virtually everything—the water bill, the gas bill, the food being gone—in fact, anything that she did not like, I was blamed for it.

The true fear of God came in while living in the home with a young woman who had three daughters of her own. Oh, my fear of having dolls in my room at night was born there, too! That house was a true home. I had my first job on a paper route. Her daughters became my sisters, and we did everything together. My father was always there. At that time, he was teaching the oldest girl how to drive, picking us up from school and taking us to the penny candy store. He treated all of us like his children. I had fun there. Although it was not my father's home or my mother's home, there was some consolation that I was secure in this woman's home. However, the Catholic school I attended terrified me. Those nuns were mean, the teacher was creepy, and we were punished for any minor infraction. I was deathly afraid of the nuns; no one wanted to fall into their hands, but somehow, I managed to do this.

They would tell you about being excommunicated and being in purgatory. They would also tell you that you had to do all the work they told you to do in order to be blessed by God. Their hamburgers were purple, their eyes glaring, and the girls were so mean and always wanted to fight. The art teacher had scary pictures on the wall of predatory animals in varying degrees of attack. The worse one was a picture of a lion ripping apart its prey. You had to stand by these photos if you were bad. How close you stood to the lion was determined by how bad you were. When you were at the lion, you got a beating with a pair of rolled up blue jeans and then the nuns would come.

One day, I ended up on these photos. In fact, majority of the class did that day. Imagine a whole bunch of fidgeting, nervous kindergarteners standing next to roaring bears and cougars. It was about seven people on the lion alone, before I even got to the lion. We all got beatings that day and the rest of the art class was spent crying in silence and coloring. I thought these people were nuts. We did nothing to deserve getting on the bear and the beatings. That's when I decided I would not listen to *any* of them. I started to rebel and got sent to the office one day with my father being called. I tore that hallway up, with all my yelling. and screaming on purpose, not because of the nuns.

The only time I enjoyed school was when the priest came to have mass and to bless us. He waved his incense about and said some words in Latin and in English. On Ash Wednesday, he placed ashes on our heads and told us that it was the mark of God or something. I did not wash my forehead for about two days because I thought the ashes would make God love me. I wanted to show Him that I loved Him and did not want to go to hell.

So, by the time I got back into my mother's custody, I was a seven-year-old hot mess. It was like being free, and I was acting out. I was also an angry, confused child. I feared everything. My mother had to deal with behaviors that I did not have when I left her. She hardly knew how to deal with me. But the spirit of fear did not stop growing in her house, nor the sense of being worthless, rebellious and fear of being blamed. That fear intensified and I acted accordingly. A lot of my problems were caused by my sense of confusion and fear within myself. But our home was stable and happy, for the most part.

While living in that home, I vowed that I would never listen or depend on anyone again. Due to my fear of authority, along with distrust, it caused a lot of self-inflicted pain, further causing me to lash out at others. Which leads me into my teenage and adult years of coping with the pain of my childhood.

Surviving in the Web

During my teenage years, I started smoking marijuana and had lost a child. I went from being an excellent student to a horrid student. I failed all my classes, but the teachers would not just put an F on my report card. My counselors kept asking me what was wrong and why was I throwing my life away. I threw away a guaranteed chance of having a music scholarship to college. My mother and my stepfather were at their wits ends, and I continued to act in rebellion.

I skipped school to smoke weed, and I became what I thought was a cool kid. However, one day in eleventh grade, two girls were sitting in front of me in Algebra, and I was high. I overheard them say, "I cannot believe it; she is high. I never would have thought she would do that. So sad," as they shook their heads with this disbelief and disgust. I felt so convicted at that moment, but I was too high to allow that comment to sink in. To this day, that comment from those girls is like a red flag for me from the Lord.

This rebellious period lasted from the time I was fifteen until I was nineteen. I hated myself and sought approval through sex. I tried to be the best friend of my friends, even though most of them did not care for me at all. All my actions were to gain assurance in myself and to please others. I wanted to join a gang because I thought I would find family and belonging. When I found out what I had to do to get in, I thought it was the stupidest idea I ever heard of!

I argued constantly with my mom, my sister was angry at me for leaving home and my dad was mad because I kept taking the car and sneaking out at night. Through all of that, I prayed and wanted to be forgiven. I tried to find out my purpose in life through Miss Cleo, a psychic, and tried to find a way to Jesus through occult means, because I was afraid to go back to the church.

I was in two abusive relationships. I was kidnapped and had to fight my way back home, almost at the cost of my life. All the time, my sense of worthlessness was growing. Since I was a little girl, I was told that I was retarded and slow. I did not believe it, but it affected the way I behaved. I wanted to show everyone that I was intelligent. I was always misunderstood by those who I needed to take me seriously. I found it difficult to fully explain my thoughts and would stutter under heavy duress.

I contemplated suicide more than once and tried to devise plans on the best way to take myself out. But when the time came for me to do the deed, I was too afraid to die. Ironically, I was afraid of God. I did not really want to die; I was convinced through the negative thinking that it would be better for my mom to not have a retarded daughter anymore. It would be better for all the world and God if I were not alive!

Ironically, around the time my father passed, which was one week before I turned twenty-one, I received salvation from my Heavenly Father. The night of my father's death, I came back home, threw my hands in the air and said, "Now, God, you can kill me. I want to go since my father is dead. You promised to take my life when my father died!" See, I had prayed to Jesus, when I was eleven that when my father died, that I would die too. I asked God to promise to take my life. And boy, did God answer my prayer—just not the way I thought He would. Hallelujah!

Destroying the Web of Fear

As a new believer in Christ trying to find my place in the church, the Lord Himself began to teach me. He taught me about forgiving myself and others. He began to show me how my emotional and mental states were defective. The more He taught me, the more understanding I achieved. The Holy Spirit taught me ways to conduct myself through the Word. There were moments in my late twenties, after much prayer, I asked the Lord God, what was truly my problem? Even though I was growing, I was growing slowly according to my estimation. I knew there were areas in my life that were stunted, and I could not find out why. That is when God showed me the spirit of fear in my life.

During my time as a "responsible" driver, I got a ticket for not stopping at a stop sign and accrued warrants for not making a court appearance to deal with that ticket. That lead to suspended license. I got tickets for driving on suspended license, and even went to jail. All of this was not because I was just being negligent, but because I was *afraid* to go to court and face the judge.

I was afraid of authority. I was afraid the judge would do what a lot of people had done — misunderstand me, twist my words, condem me, confound me and punish me. One day, I prayed and asked the Lord to make the tickets go away. He told me I needed to go to the court and face the judge. I told Him I was scared, that I would lose everything and end up in jail for many years. He told me to not be afraid, that He was with me and to trust Him. He said the judges would respect me because I came to them, instead of being arrested again.

I decided to do as God had instructed. I went to the first judge, and yes, I was still afraid. The voices in my head kept me in constant fear. The voices told me that I was a goner, that I was going to be locked up that day because of my warrants, and that I would lose my home and my job. I kept moving through the fear and reminded myself of the words of the Lord and what He told me to do.

That day was a huge victory for me over fear. I walked into the court and walked out! The judge said he was glad I came. He said he would work with me and he reduced my fees. I went to two other judges, and they both showed me mercy. I was so glad because I had victory over my fear of authority. I got so used to coming to court to meet my obligations, I showed up happily to court one day. After sitting there for some time, the judge said, "Ms. Morgan, why are you here?"

"I came to see you; I have a court date," I responded. The judge started laughing.

"Today is not your day, and I do not think you have to come back to see me at all. See, if half of y'all showed up like Ms. Morgan here, you could save yourself money and jail time. Ms. Morgan, go and visit the window and see if you have another date."

I smiled; it felt so good knowing that the judge knew me by name—not because I was repeating an offense, but that I was showing up to make sure I was not in offense. That day, the judge waived the rest of my fees and gave me the "all clear". That gave me courage to deal with any other authority figure in my life from that point on, even with their criticism, whether good or bad.

On that day, I was truly delivered from the fear of authority, because the Lord used that judge to show how He operates in mercy to those who seek Him. In and out of offense, in joy and in love. I overcame the fear of abandonment simply by building my relationship with Christ over the years and trusting Him in the most wounded areas of my life. No longer was God a lightning-throwing God, but one of love, healing, mercy and kindness.

Gone was the rage and anger because I forgave myself and others. Gone was the addiction, because I got the courage to deal head on with my emotions and the pain. Gone was my fear of being retarded and stupid because the Lord reaffirmed me in Himself. His Word is in full effect in my life. Even in 2020, I faced one of my over-arching fears, which is fear of losing my home and my belongings. I was truly afraid; the first few days I could not sleep at all. I wept, prayed and pleaded with the Lord, not understanding why I was placed in this situation—even though I was responsible. The Lord reminded me of all the circumstances He brought me through and how He did not abandon me. He told me to trust Him. I did, and in the eleventh hour and hardly any money, God made a way for me to move into another home. My friends came to help me move.

So even through this pandemic, through the layoff of my job, and faced with not being able to go back to work as a driver, I am at peace. I can truly say that I am not afraid. Once I got over being at the brink of losing everything, I realized when this pandemic happened, there will be no fear in me nor my home. I will encourage my friends and family to not fear.

As I have stated earlier in this chapter, breaking the web of fear is not easy. It requires one to be honest about their fear and to have courage to confront it. We must be able to realize how fear is controlling our lives and to work through it with the Holy Spirit. The start of breaking the demonic foundation of fear is to replace it with the fear of the Lord, which is respect, love and obedience. It takes courage to be obedient to the Word of God and to not fall back into old habits when confronted with stressful situations. Fear needs to feed off and build its web. It takes absolute trust in God to destroy that web. Although it's scary, we must depend wholly on the Lord and not our own wisdom, knowledge, power, authority, money or abilities. Trusting wholly in God does not tie your hands from doing anything, but releases you from the burden that many carry today. It allows you to refocus on what is truly important instead of trying to fear control by providing solution to a situation you barely have a grasp on.

Remember the spirit of fear is the opposite of the spirit that God gives. Instead of power, fear makes us powerless, weak, cowardly and ineffective. Instead of love, fear creates rage and anger and hate. Instead of a sound mind, fear creates paranoia, deception and disillusionment. The Spirit that God gives us is His Holy Spirit, which brings power and love and a sound mind. Destroying that web is like peeling an onion, layer by layer. The Lord can deliver you all at once, but He knows that it is more like surgery; bit by bit, you are delivered because He wants you to work and learn to trust Him in the midst of your fears and terror so you can understand how this spirit is controlling and defeating you.

In conclusion, please understand that the enemy wants you afraid because he is afraid of you and of your assured and potential victory through the Christ. I say assured because the kingdom of darkness has already been defeated by Jesus. All those who trust in Him and follow Him will assuredly have victory. I say potential because it is a choice to choose to trust Jesus. It is not something you are forced to do, yet it is eternally beneficial for you to do so.

The benefits of trusting Christ will be experienced in this life and the one to come. Those who have the Spirit of Christ, have authority and power over the demonic spirits. Therefore, we can destroy the works of the kingdom of darkness in our own lives and others. There is hope. I overcame many fears in my life through understanding, trusting in God and courage. I pray that my testimony will give you the boldness to overcome whatever fear, phobia or terror that is keeping you from being a fruitful servant of Christ!

About the Author

Anita F. Morgan is an author, ordained minister and the founder of Grace Redeemed Me Ministry, where she is called to reach, teach, prepare and encourage the people of God. A native of Detroit, Michigan, Anita completed her bachelor's and master's degrees in theology from Destiny Christian University. Driven by her love of the Lord and passion for the lost, Anita has served in various ministries over the years including serving the sick and shut-in at various nursing and rehabilitation facilities.

Overcoming the Fear of Rejection

By Brian A. Matthews

My story begins as a little boy who was confronted with the unfamiliar. I was facing time away from my mother. I can't recall how many years she was gone, but I do know that she was gone for quite a while. When she returned, I was expecting something totally different from what I received. Adjusting to things being different was okay because my mom was back, and we were going to be one, big happy family. Or so I thought.

I was unaware of the spirit of rejection that was being set up in my life. I had no idea what rejection was, what it felt like or that it could come from someone who I loved with my whole heart. All I knew was that I missed my mom and I just wanted her attention. Now mind you, I'm looking at this from a six-year-old's perspective. I wasn't thinking about the "grown up" things that she was dealing with. She was pregnant. But you see, in my childlike mentality, her pregnancy wasn't my concern. Nope! Not at all! All I thought was, *You're home. I missed you. You're supposed to be giving me all the attention that I wasn't getting while you were away.*

Welp, that is not the way it went down. Not even close. It seemed like all of her time revolved around the new baby. Yaaaay! (insert sarcasm). I guess the new baby was way more important. Sounds like I was being kind of selfish, huh? Who was I to want my mom's undivided attention? It wasn't like she was gone for just about *five years* or anything. I loved my little sister; but right now, she was interfering with *my quality time* with *my* mother.

There were so many things that I didn't know about that were about to put a stranglehold on me emotionally, spiritually *and* mentally. Here I am, a kid dealing with envy all because the one woman who I wanted attention from constantly rejected me. Man, if only I knew then what I know now. One thing that I learned was that my thoughts of what life should be and what was reality were two different things. This spirit of rejection was setting me up on the road to rebellion.

The spirit of rejection wasn't detected early in my life. As a result, it grew into one serious monster. Just imagine how things were when I got older with that spirit of rejection still hanging around, whispering negative thoughts that haunted me throughout my preteen and adolescent years. So many times, I felt rejected by my mom and was unable to express what was going inside my head. Even though I was hurting, I kept everything to myself and harbored a lot of anger and resentment. Did that affect my relationship with my sister? A lil' bit. It was rough for a minute, but we're good now.

Now that I've told you a little bit about how the fear of rejection entered through my relationship with my mom. Let me show you how it continued to rear its ugly head through my relationship with my dad.

So, I'll start by saying that my dad was fifteen when he impregnated my mom. Can you guess what was his birthday present for his sixteenth birthday? Yep, you guessed it. *Me!* How's that for a birthday gift? So, get this. His parents sent him away, refusing to believe that he was the father of this child out of wedlock. Guess who grew up without his father? Yep, you guessed it again! This guy. So fast forward to me being around ten or eleven years old. I remember this day so clearly. I had been begging my mom to take me to see my dad. She finally gave in and took me to see him.

Wouldn't you know that I wanted to stay with him? I was crying because my mom said that there was no way that she was letting me stay with him. Welp, he came to the car, saw me crying and told my mom that there's no way that I could be his son because he don't make crybabies. Talk about heartbreak and rejection. Okay, so let's fast forward to the age of fifteen where two specific moments stood out.

1. He saw me and my mom at the Farmer Jack grocery store that used to be on 12th Street in the Virginia Park Shopping

Plaza. You would've thought that he saw a ghost from how fast he ran up out of there. By the way, he was with his wife, Carol. Made me wonder if he had even told her that he had an older child.

2. He used to shoot pool at this pool hall that was around the corner from us when we stayed on Vancourt Street. We found this out because my Uncle Tony told us. Welp, he decided to mosey on around there to see me, but get this. He had the *audacity* to tell my mother that she was messing up his money and that she had to *pay* him to spend time with me.

That was my eye-opening moment with him. I was so hurt that this man who I wanted to be in my life so badly, rejected me right to my face. I was so angry and hurt, so I made up my mind that I wouldn't seek anything else from him. I did get back in touch with him at an older age, but that rejection demon had already set up shop. I had a hard time accepting him back, even though by this time, he had become a pastor.

Believe me, I love my parents; however, the scar I have from their rejection had me in a bad place. I mean, *they* were *my* parents! And yet, they couldn't find it anywhere in their hearts to show me that I was important to them. I had some very uncomfortable talks with them once I came of age and understood what was going on spiritually. I'll get to that later on.

I wasn't even aware of the fact that my fear of rejection caused serious problems in my social life. How? I'm glad that you asked. I was so afraid of being rejected, that I was afraid to move. I was afraid to ask. I was just plain afraid. It became even worse when I was allowed to go outside and talk to other people in my age group. It was so awkward. I really didn't know what to do or how to interact with other people, especially the opposite sex. Man, I had no clue how to hold a conversation.

My fear of rejection was so strong that I developed this new persona. I started lying to be able to fit in. Well, that didn't work too well, because nearly everyone knew my mother and that in itself, didn't help at all. She found ways to embarrass me in some shape, form or fashion. It didn't help that I was a funny-looking kid when I was growing up. I was mixture of "J.J. Evans" from *Good Times* and "Roger Thomas" from *What's Happening!!* Big lips. Big glasses. Super skinny. Peasy hair. All bad. Getting rejected by girls was a regular event for me.

The spirit of rejection engulfed me to the point that I was angry, afraid, hurt and sad, just to name a few. I couldn't understand why no one liked me. What had I done that caused no one to want to give me the basic thing that I wanted: Attention. Little did I know, but I was about to get some attention alright—but not the kind that I wanted. I started acting out as an adolescent. I wanted my mother's attention so bad that my behavior got a little out of control. My mother got me together real quick.

By now, I was becoming more interested in girls and I found myself looking for companionship to help me deal with the rejection that I was getting at home. Well, that didn't work out well either. I forgot that I was the "ugly duckling" and there was no way any girl in her right mind would want to be seen with me—let alone talk to me. Are you kidding? I got tricked and played so many times because girls thought it would be funny to pretend that they liked me, and then "breakup" with me in front of a group of kids for being ugly or stupid.

I was a very sensitive child, so my feelings got hurt easily. This rejection thing had me feeling some kind of way. I never told anyone that I had thoughts of suicide as a kid. Remember, I said that I kept everything to myself. Mentally, I just hid myself away and learned how to pretend that everything was good. The enemy was stringing me along and I was willfully following.

That fear of rejection had me feeling like no one wanted me around. I felt like it would if I had followed through on my thoughts of suicide then it would have been as if I had never been born. In these moments, I assumed that no one knew how far the spirit of rejection could take you if you allowed it to consume you. Being filled with rejection caused me to develop an extremely negative attitude. I wouldn't ask for help or look for jobs or anything. I pretty much gave up. What I didn't know was that God had people praying for me and planting seeds in my spirit that were going to manifest later. I just had to get to the assigned place that He had destined for me. I was so busy moping along through life that I didn't even know that a Man, who had been rejected by His own people despite His unconditional love for them, was getting ready to introduce Himself to me.

You see, the enemy had me so gone that I *almost* gave up. But God! God showed me that He hadn't given up on me and that I had an assignment. So fast forward to later in life. Remember when I said that I had to have uncomfortable conversations with my parents? This is that moment.

My mother was understanding. We were able to get through the tears and even laughter to come to an understanding about our mother/son relationship. Now my dad, that was a different story. He, like most men, had a difficult time admitting that he was wrong about anything. So the conversation was okay; however, it was strained. What I learned from Dad was, "men don't get emotional like that; well, they shouldn't". God showed me something different. God showed me that in order to get to the next level, you must be healed *and* made whole. Those two things go hand in hand. I thank God that He loved me enough to show me that His love is unconditional and that He will never leave nor forsake me.

Because of the Word I know now that I am no longer controlled by the spirit of rejection. I had to learn who I am in Christ and that the enemy has no power over me. As long as I know that the Lord is with me, guiding me through the valley, I have no need to fear *anything*. Amen and thank you Jesus!

About the Author

A moving conversationalist with a compelling story to tell, Brian A. Matthews inspires people in the midst of his life's toughest challenges. Working through and rising out of the grips of poverty on the rough streets of Detroit, Brian draws on his captivating life story to change the narrative on inner-city culture and the plight of the African American male.

Overcoming the Fear of Self-Rejection

By Tatrice M. Starks

"Your value doesn't decrease based on someone's inability to see your value."

Rejection is the dismissing or refusing of a proposal, idea or a person. It comes in the form of non-acceptance, abandonment, exclusion, ostracism, and excommunication. Other forms include being blacklisted, black balled, or simply brushed off. Rejection shows its ugly head at birth. The baby is slapped on their behind and handed over to his or her mother. Mother then makes the first assessment of this newborn. Not even a half hour out of labor, the mother and father both ask a series of questions: *Is he (or she) perfect? Does he (or she) have all his (her) fingers and toes? Who does he (or she) look like?*

I believe that Mommy, Daddy and every form of spiritual wickedness are present at birth. The Bible calls Satan a thief who comes to steal, kill and destroy (John 10:10). The enemy doesn't care what tactic he uses to destroy you as long as the job is completed.

Satan's playground is in your mind. If he can make you have self-defeating, self-loathing, self-destructive thoughts about yourself, that's what he will use. The Bible calls him *the father of lies* (John 8:44). If he can get into your thoughts or use the people around you to harm you, that is his master plan!

Satan devised a plan to destroy Jesus at His birth. *Kill all the first born!* I believe he does not change his methods because it has worked for him for thousands of years. *Stop them early,* he decreed, *so that they will not grow up to be everything God called them to be. Toy with their minds. Kill them!*

I dealt with rejection as a young child! My parents were pastors, so I was a "P.K.," an acronym for "Pastor's Kid." The title P.K. alone has its own ugly form of rejection. Whenever I made mention that I was the daughter of pastors, without fail, I was met with negativity.

"Oh, you gotta watch out for those preacher's kids because they are the worst!" I was judged by older adults, family, teachers, ex-boyfriends and *church folk.* I purposefully italicized church folk. I thought that the church house was a place of restoration, where one should feel safe and loved! Unfortunately, the church is where I felt judged and ridiculed. In my lifetime, I think I became the "poster child" for experiencing the most rejection. In elementary school, I was teased about my name, Tatrice. My name was often misspelled and mispronounced. One of my teachers changed my name from Ta-Trice to "TaT-Rice." I loved her dearly; however, every time she called my name for class participation, I wanted to hide under my desk because the children would erupt into a chorus of laughter and jokes.

Sadly, the ridicule always came from the boys I had a crush on. I was too young and underdeveloped at the time. I didn't own enough courage to defend my name or have a conversation with my teacher to let her know how I felt when she toyed with the pronunciation of my name. To this day, she still pronounces my name wrong, but now I understand that it was a term of endearment. But for the record, Mrs. B., my name is *Tatrice*.

My self-confidence was limp and I was defenseless. In the dispensation I grew up in, children were seen and not heard. In other words, we could *not* talk to adults about who or what bothered us. In the meantime, we were touched, sexually molested, punched, pinched, slapped, mishandled and ridiculed. If by chance someone did listen to your accusations, you would face being blackballed or labeled as a liar. So, many of us suffered in silence as victims at the hands of our fathers, uncles, aunties, your momma's best friend and the babysitter. I also survived a bully in my classroom. The bully saw that I was vulnerable, so she took advantage of my defenseless personality.

Parents, pay attention to your children. A lot can happen in the elementary school classroom. Be available to listen to your children's stories. Listen to their daily interactions; let your child know that you are available to them and for them, no matter what. The Bible states it's the little foxes that destroy the vine (Song of Solomon 2:15).

Unfortunately, I struggled with being humiliated about my name. I also had to defend my looks and my body shape type. Little did I know that adult family members would be the worst critics. I was often compared to my siblings. I was told I was not as attractive or as talented as my siblings. My efforts to sing were dismantled. I was afraid to use my God-given ability to sing. I often heard comments like, "You sing like your mother, wow!" My mom looked like Dionne Warwick, but she sure did not sound like her. My siblings were compared to singing like my father, who had a voice like the late Donny Hathaway. I assumed I sounded like Miss Piggy singing to Kermit.

Speaking of Miss Piggy, I was often called "Burtha Butt." I was ostracized for my body type. Comments were made about me like, "Look at her, trying to be grown with all that tail." The tribe of women around me belittled my body type, which caused me to be ashamed of my natural maturation and growth into a young woman. Instead of being celebrated and welcomed into womanhood, I was made to feel like a freak or a thot.

I vividly recall my cousin's birthday party one Saturday. My family members were outside in the yard celebrating his birthday. The adults were talking, food was on the grill and music filled the air. I wanted to get in the kiddie pool, but I had forgotten my swimsuit. One of my aunts allowed me to borrow her swimwear. She gave me the baddest swimsuit in her wardrobe, and I was excited! I ran in the house, straight upstairs into the bathroom to put the stunning black swimsuit on.

It was revealing and low cut. Plain, downright *sexy*. I filled out every inch of that swimsuit. I looked in the mirror on the back of the bathroom door, and I loved what I saw. I placed my hands on my hips and for a moment, I was a supermodel. Although I was only fourteen or fifteen at the time, I had the body of an adult woman. I felt a little uncomfortable, but the swimsuit looked so nice on me.

It was 90 degrees on that hot, sunny August day. When I stepped in that backyard, I experienced something straight out of the horror movie "Carrie." I felt like a lamb going to the slaughter. I placed my towel on the chair and got into the pool with all the other children. I noticed the looks on the elder women in the yard. They looked at me and whispered amongst themselves.

"She knows that swimsuit is too grown for her!" one of them whispered with indignation. Out the corner of my eye, I also noticed one of the neighbors admiring what he saw without any discernment for my adolescence. In my mind, he licked his lips like the Big Bad Wolf from *The Three Little Pigs*. Immediately, I felt anxious, sad and harmed. I wished I had worn a T-shirt over the beautiful, too-sexy frock. I felt ashamed! I jumped out the pool, grabbed my beach towel and sat in the chair for the rest of the day. I vowed to never show my body again.

When the time came to talk about important topics such as sex and the human body, I shunned the thought of that being a natural process in life. I thought I was fat, nasty, a thot, untalented and not good enough. Fashion for plus-sized women in the 1980s and 90s was horrible. I was a curvy, voluptuous, plus-sized girl, and I was ashamed about that. I was told I looked like my Dad's sisters. My interpretation of that at the time was *I was fat and unacceptable*. I suffered for a long time with low self-esteem and depression. So, I decided to camouflage my body by wearing black *everything*. The words and ridicule of "TaT-Rice" followed me from my childhood and adolescence straight into my adult life. It plagued me for years.

I loved me a fine, black, tall, athletic-built man — especially in high school. I was specifically in love with my high school quarterback, and he was a freshman! I was also in love with the quarterback from the year ahead of us. I secretly stalked them both. I felt like I had so many strikes against me, they did not give me the time of day. I thought to myself, *if I wasn't so fat and unattractive, maybe I could get their attention.* In high school, my hormones were all over the place. I just wanted a boyfriend; so I devised a plan.

I decided to wear my "Holy Ghost Jesus" outfits out the door to school so my parents wouldn't look at me sideways. After school, I had my *School Daze* biker shorts and a tight shirt in my locker. I just had to remember to change back by the time I got back to the "preachers' house." The biker shorts got their attention; however, I soon realized that they wanted *more* than a church kiss and to grind on clothes. My church taught me to save myself for my husband. I was a virgin, and I was not ready to go any further than that.

After high school, I met and married my husband. My husband had an athletic-build with curly hair. I didn't have to worry anymore about not being attractive to men. Or so I thought. I brought all of the baggage from my past into my marriage. I learned that marriage had its own set of problems—*big* problems. Arguments, immaturity and surprises; we were unprepared and ill-advised. Being in love was not enough! Marriage sent me into an abyss of darkness and depression. Things got so bad between us, and I noticed how my husband was coming home later and later. I turned to what I knew: Self-hatred. If I never fully embraced and loved myself, how could I possibly survive marriage?

I fell into depression because I had placed all of my treasure into this man. My expectations were grandiose. I needed him to love me, provide for me and meet my every need. I went to work, came home, laid in the bed in darkness and cried myself to sleep. While lying in bed, I often heard voices. The voices would say things like, *Kill yourself...no one loves you...you're ugly, fat, unattractive...you have no purpose.* There's a constant tennis match for your mind! The Bible says that to whom you yield yourself, you become the servant of (Romans 6:16). You can't defeat those thoughts if you do not stay connected to the Holy Spirit. Pray and read your Word. *Why does rejection matter? Why does what people say about you matter?*

Life and death are in the power of the tongue (Proverbs 18:21). You must protect your eye gates and your ear gates from negative words because words have power! James 3:5-6 (NIV) says, *Likewise, the tongue is a small part of the body, but it makes great boasts. Consider what a great forest is set on fire by a small spark. The tongue also is a fire, a world of evil among the parts of the body. It corrupts the whole body, sets the whole course of one's life on fire, and is itself set on fire by hell!* James 3:8 says, *but no human being can tame the tongue. It is a restless evil, full of deadly poison.*

Mark 11:23b NKJV declares that you can "...believe that those things which he says will be done, he will have whatever he says". You can also have whatsoever *other people* say to you if you don't catch the words, filter and cast them down. You also become whatever you *hear*. It goes like this: Words goes into your ear, from your ear to your heart, from the heart your mind and soul embodies it becomes a real thing.

I suffered from low self-esteem and a lack of body acceptance. I often heard negative conversations about my weight and my shape. When I started working at Lane Bryant, I had an "A-ha!" moment. I realized that plus-sized, curvy girls can look great and flaunt who they are with *confidence!* Working in an environment where it's okay to accept yourself — no matter what size you are, changed my perception of *myself* immediately. After working at Lane Bryant and being in an environment of acceptance, I changed my mindset to, *what if this applies to me? What if everyone who said the terrible things about me didn't like themselves? What if they were insecure and they wanted that insecurity for me?*

I discovered a few things while working at Lane Bryant:

Most curvy girls have the prettiest faces. It's okay to jiggle when you walk. Curvy women can wear whatever they want to, as long as they believe they can. Just because you are plus-sized doesn't mean you can't be trendy. Curvy women wear their clothes with the most confidence. The curvy woman doesn't mind spending top dollar to look good.

I gained confidence and self-acceptance while being employed at Lane Bryant. I emerged out of my shell of wearing all black, to a vibrant, colorful fashionista - hair done, nails done, clothes popping. The truth is I needed to see another reality, other than the one previously spoken over me. What may have started as the fear of rejection has given me acceptance in who God created me to be and I love who I am!

About the Author

Born and raised in Philadelphia, Pennsylvania, Tatrice M. Starks is blessed with the magnificent gift of creating a warm space for women to express themselves and live comfortably in their own skin. Founder of ESP4HER, Tatrice is a powerhouse influencer who builds her life around the 4Ms – motherhood, ministry, modeling and motivational speaking. Tatrice has evolved from feeling invisible as a child into an unforgettable woman of purpose and a serial entrepreneur. Through experience, she's learned that life is all about being who God created you to be and *not* who the world thinks you should be. Standing boldly in her faith, Tatrice is committed to inspiring other women and girls to live a purpose-driven life.

Overcoming the Fear of Failure

By Dr. Mary K. Clark

Our deepest fear is not that we are inadequate.

Our deepest fear is that we are powerful beyond measure.

It is our light, not our darkness

That most frightens us. ~Marianne Williamson

Who Am I?

There were many significant instances in my life when the opinions and judgment of others reflected their lack of faith in my ability to succeed. Each incident could have easily ignited a fire of fear inside of me, resulting in a disastrous outcome. Instead of accepting the fear of others, each attempted blow to my spirit actually fueled my determination to succeed. My saving grace was the confidence my parents instilled in me and my siblings. Because of that confidence, I did not believe the doubters. Mom did not accept us saying, "I can't." She told us to either figure it out or ask for help; but we should never let, "I can't" be the reason not to try. To this day, when I hear someone I know say "I can't," I ask them if they choose not to do it or if they are unable to do it? If they say they are unable, I try to help them or find someone who can.

So, let me just lay these situations on the table and I'll unpack each to show how each situation formed me into the strong, determined person I am today.

1. High school honors were taken away *the day before* graduation.

2. Professor in my master's program subtly accused me of plagiarizing an interview that I conducted with a successful black female entrepreneur.

3. Doctoral admissions were denied because of my GRE scores.

I am a black woman and that will never change. It's the first thing you see when you see me. What has and will continue to change are the labels and perceptions of what those labels represent to those I meet. Here's a quick review of a few labels used to describe me — *to my face* — over my 64 years: Colored, black, African American, n-word, Black n-word, Black b****, and n-word b**** and doctor, just to name a few. Fortunately, some of those less flattering and derogatory labels do not define who I was or who I have become. What the labels do provide was a representation of how I've been categorized by others.

At times, some of those labels caused discomfort and anger; at other times, those labels caused sadness. What I have grown to understand is that each time a negative or derogatory label was thrown at me, my invisible armor grew stronger. That armor, also known as "thick skin," has served me well and protected me throughout my life. My armor has been instrumental in helping me overcome the fear that could have crippled me many times throughout my life.

I grew up on a 40-acre farm in rural America. I lived in Arbela Township, a 33.5 square mile area. With a current population of just over 3,200, Arbela Township is a rural residential and agricultural community, located in the southwest portion of Tuscola County in the thumb area of Michigan. It is about twenty-five minutes northeast of Flint. Our community was closely associated with the village of Millington, which is how our mail was postmarked. So, when asked where I grew up, my response was Millington. My home, on the corner of Arbela and Barkley Roads, was always a safe haven for me. This is where my experiences were centered for the first seventeen years of my life, until I left for college in 1974.

My father's family moved to Millington in the early 1920s to a 120-acre farm. At that time, they were the only black family in Millington. My father had four brothers and two sisters. My mother grew up in Vassar, another small town near Saginaw, where my father would visit as a young man. They met and married in 1951 and had four children: one boy and three girls. I was the next to the youngest. My father purchased a 40-acre farm less than a mile from where he was raised. By the time I entered grade school, there were at least three more black families in the area. I was the only black person out of a graduating class of 158 students. It's one of those small towns where everyone knew everyone else or was familiar with the family.

Many of the families owned and operated farms which produced dairy, beef, wheat, corn, cucumbers and other produce. Migrant workers would come to the area each summer and harvest produce growing on some of the large farms. The community had many generations of families of German and Polish descent. Some residents were employed at the local automobile factories either in Flint or Saginaw. It was a small, respectable community that was predominantly white.

As a high school student in the early 70s, I knew I wanted to go to college. My father was a college graduate, and I spoke with him about his college experience many times. During the 9th and 10th grades, I regularly visited the guidance counselor's office lobby where all of the college information was displayed. Many of my breaks between classes were spent in the counselor's office lobby, looking at brochures and reading about various professions in the world. Who would I be when I grow up? Where would I go to college? What would it take for me to sit down and talk with the counselor?

I didn't know how to make an appointment or if that was even allowed. I saw "popular" students enter and leave the counselor's office. At first, I thought it was only the older students—the juniors and seniors, who were allowed into that mysterious office I'd never entered. How did they get invited into the "inner sanctum" of the guidance counselor? What did I need to do to get invited to sit and talk about my future college plans? When I realized that some of my classmates also had an opportunity to meet with the counselor, I was determined to do the same.

I finally got the nerve to approach the guidance counselor for an appointment. To my surprise, she acknowledged knowing me. *Great*, I thought. She knows who I am. Right there in the lobby, she proceeded to give me my two-minute counseling session. Her recommendation was that I consider a vocational training program because I was best suited to be a secretary or a factory worker, based on the aptitude test we had been given. *What?* I thought to myself.

A "secretary." That had never crossed my mind as a career, although it's a respectable option for anyone who desires that profession. I had aspirations to attend college. I envisioned myself teaching or working in an industry that involved numbers because I enjoyed math. I enjoyed the precision that numbers represented. Initially her recommendation offended me. Later, I was enraged that she made such an unfair judgment of my abilities based on an aptitude test. My invisible armor grew stronger that day.

I never went back to that counselor. On that day, I learned that I would have to be my own guidance counselor. I went to the library, looked at reference books and contacted colleges directly. This was decades before the Internet and Google. I continued to visit the lobby area of the counselor's office to look at any new brochures about colleges and scholarships. I would send for college catalogs and additional information.

I found some information about a pre-college day trip to Western Michigan University (WMU) in the counselor's lobby display. I asked my parents if I would be allowed to go based on the information I found. When an opportunity presented itself for students interested in WMU to take a bus trip to Kalamazoo, Mom and Dad said yes, and I was on my way to explore the campus and learn what college life was about. I liked what I saw and early in my senior year, I applied for admission and eagerly awaited the decision.

I had only one other college as a comparison. That was General Motors Institute (GMI), which is now Kettering University, a small private campus in the heart of Flint where my cousin, Brenda attended. WMU was the only campus visit

I attended, although I applied to several other universities. I was ultimately offered admission to Western Michigan University. I knew that it was going to be a financial challenge for the family, so I told my parents I would see if I was eligible for a student loan at the local bank in Millington.

And Now the Good News. Not!

I was eager to begin college in the fall; but prior to graduating, another experience potentially destroyed my spirit. It was June 5, 1974, the day before graduation. The thought of seeing my classmates together for the final time had us filled with excitement. I was surprised to receive a telephone call from Mr. Peterson, the high school principal. This had to be a really big deal. I had never received a personal call from one of the administrators.

My excitement was quickly destroyed. Mr. Peterson informed me that I had received an "E" on my World History final exam, which lowered my grade in that class from a "B" to a "C." That wasn't the end of his news. That "C" in World History lowered my overall grade point average to a 2.95, which fell below the minimum of 3.0 GPA that's required for honors students. He went on to explain that I no longer qualified as an honor student. My name would be removed from the list of those graduating with honors, and I had to return my honor cords prior to the graduation ceremony.

What he didn't do was ask if something happened to cause me to fail the exam so miserably. I earned mostly A's and a few B's in my other classes. It troubled me that the instructor didn't reach out. I never saw the graded final exam, so I always had doubts about what really happened. I was filled with so many emotions that day, but the overwhelming emotion was embarrassment.

On graduation day, I discreetly turned in my honor cords before the ceremony. I didn't mention what happened to anyone, not even my parents. I hoped that no one would say anything. I glanced at the program and noticed that my name did not have an asterisk designating those graduating with honors. When my name, "Mary K. Clark," was called, the words, "with honors," did not publicly accompany my name as it did with my other classmates with honors. From that experience, my invisible armor grew a bit thicker.

According to my student record, I ranked thirty-five out of a graduating class of 158 students; however, after the phone call from the principal, if my spirit was a student in our class, it was at the lowest ranking possible of 159. Through four years of high school, I had four teachers who acknowledged my potential and made me know I could be successful. Those teachers were Anne Hutchins, Harry Kern, Barbara Metiva, and Richard Murphy. None of them ever knew how I felt as I left Millington High School and never went back.

There were many positive highlights in my high school experience. I developed strong leadership skills. I learned how to excel in the face of almost daily challenges and barriers. I was in my mid-40s when I finally shared the information about the call from Mr. Peterson on the eve of my graduation, with my parents. I had achieved sufficient success in my life to offset the low point that I experienced as a teenager. To say that my father was furious is the biggest understatement one could ever make. My father didn't curse; but on that day, in the thought bubble above his head, I saw words and phrases that I could not imagine coming from this pillar of the community. He was ready to kick a whole bunch of asses and take a legal pad full of names. That's my interpretation of what I saw. He was a man on fire. How dare someone (some 30 years ago) disgrace his baby without explanation? He was going to get to the bottom of that mess.

Well, I was able to calm Dad down. I let him know that I had worked my way through all of the emotions he just expressed and there was no need to contact anyone. At that point, Mr. Peterson was still living and I know my father was about to call him and give him a tongue lashing from which he may not have recovered. It became my father's mission in life to rectify the situation in some way. He was so proud of all of my educational and professional accomplishments. He went on a one-man campaign to get me invited as the featured speaker at a Millington High School commencement. Unfortunately, he was not able to achieve his wish for me to give a commencement speech before his death in 2002.

When I left Millington, I had gained an invisible coat of armor (i.e. thick skin) that provided emotional protection throughout my life. I attended Western Michigan University for three years until April 1977 when I decided to take a break from my education and get married.

You're in the Army Now, Kind of...

Before our marriage in July 1977, I had some important commitments to fulfill. In August of the previous year, I enlisted for a three-year tour of duty in the Army Reserves, along with two of my girlfriends, Gayle and Gerbie. The commitment was manageable. I had to report for duty one weekend per month and two weeks a year for summer camp. Because I enlisted right before I returned to school in September 1976, my Army Basic Training also known as "boot camp" was delayed until the following year. I was required to complete two weeks of summer camp in May 1977 at Fort Knox, Kentucky. Prior to leaving for summer camp, I received my official orders to report to Fort McClellan in Anniston, Alabama for Basic Training in June. So in early June 1977, for the first time in my life, I reluctantly boarded an airplane at Bishop Airport in Flint and I was off for an unknown boot camp adventure somewhere in Alabama.

I arrived at boot camp as a 155-pound bride-to-be with my wedding day quickly approaching in less than forty-five days. I didn't have a clue what lay ahead for me. There were others on the flight headed to boot camp and our group was the last to arrive at the base. As a result, as soon as we arrived, we met with those who had arrived earlier. We obtained our housing assignments, were measured for clothing and equipment and directed to our barracks to settle in.

Here's the short version of the story: Days two and three, we went through what was to become our daily routine: got up very early, made our beds, quickly ate our meals, and did a lot of sitting and waiting. Because the heat and humidity level were so high, we were prohibited from doing any activity or physical training outside at the risk of heat stroke and overexertion. By day four when the heat subsided, I was notified that I was five pounds over the allowable weight by military standards for someone of my age. I was given two options. Option number one: Lose five or more pounds within two days at the base. Option number two: Return home, lose weight and return to Basic Training at a later date once I have achieved the desired weight.

Let me get this straight, had I just been told I was too fat to complete Basic Training? Well, I had some time to think about my decision during my overnight shift staffing the reception desk at the barracks. The following morning, although tired, my mind was clear enough to make a definite decision. I was a bride-to-be with less than forty-one days until my wedding. The last thing I wanted to stress over for the next two days was whether or not I would succeed or fail in attaining the allowable weight standards for the Army. I gave the commanding officer my decision, packed my bags with lightning speed, said goodbye to fellow soldiers who I knew I would never see again, and I was homeward bound. I never looked back.

I always had a faint nagging feeling of failure in the back of my mind for being singled out for excess weight. Consequently, 155 pounds was the lowest weight I've been in my entire adult life. I haven't been anywhere close to that weight since that incident. My invisible armor grew a bit thicker the day I left. I completed my three-year enlistment in the Army Reserves. I was not required to return to complete

Basic Training during my commitment. I received an honorable discharge at the conclusion of my three years and that was the end of my Army Reserves career.

Here Comes the Bride, There Goes the Bride

We got married in July 1977. I worked as a bank teller while my husband completed his degree at General Motors Institute. We lived in Flint until my husband graduated in 1979. I was determined to return to complete my degree. After my husband graduated, we moved to Bowling Green, Ohio, which was a reasonable commute to his job in Defiance, Ohio. We lived within walking distance to Bowling Green State University, where I transferred my previous credits and enrolled in a Fashion Merchandising program. I began classes in January 1980 and completed my bachelor's degree two years later, while our marriage was slowly deteriorating.

As I was being a dutiful wife and student, things were happening that were slowly revealed to me in unexpected ways. For example, as I paid the monthly bills, I discovered a credit card receipt for a flat tire repair which happened when my husband met a random woman in Cincinnati. Another random woman was discovered keeping my husband company in our apartment while I was in Atlanta attending my first national convention of my sorority. Then there was the random woman that my husband professed his undying love to in a letter that I discovered on the front seat of our car one morning as I prepared to go grocery shopping. He eventually moved out in November 1981.

I didn't share this drama with anyone, especially my family. I didn't want them to worry. He agreed to pay the household bills. I was in my final two semesters and unemployed. I was 100% financially dependent on him. I made a mental note that a dependency like this will never happen again. My armor just got a little thicker.

He even made an appearance as the devoted husband during my graduation activities when more than twenty family members and friends joined to celebrate the occasion in the spring of 1982. After all of the festivities had passed, I told my family that we were separated. I began looking for a job. I moved from Bowling Green to Flint to live with my sister. By September, I landed my first job at Winkelman's in Flint as an assistant store manager utilizing my fashion merchandising degree.

Over the next two years of my career at Winkelman's, I continued to take on more responsibility as I worked in Flint, Lansing, Chicago, and Detroit. I was sent to various locations because of my ability to quickly turn challenging situations into successful operations. I was transferred to Winkelman's in Northland Mall in Detroit, one of the largest and most successful stores within the chain.

From there, I was promoted to manage a very small, old and somewhat dangerous location of Winkelman's on Gratiot Avenue near East 8 Mile Road in Detroit. Seeking safety and greater responsibility, I applied to and was hired by Lane Bryant where I worked for nine months until a better opportunity was presented by Casual Corner, another retail clothing store. So, off I went to Southland Mall in August 1985. I was ready for an exciting opportunity as assistant manager with the promise of a promotion as manager of my own store in the near future.

My personal life was in a state of quiet turmoil. I had separated from my husband more than three years earlier. My meager salary was around $20,000 annually. I didn't know how much a divorce would cost, but I was certain it was more than I could presently afford. At the time, he was not willing to pay for or contribute to the cost of dissolving our tattered marriage. I had no thought of dating for many reasons, mainly because my trust in what a loving relationship represents was destroyed. Also, I was uncomfortable entering into another relationship until the current one was over. I just wanted out.

Whatever the sacrifice, I was determined to save enough money to hire an attorney so I could put this failed relationship behind me and move the hell on. It angered me that my soon-to-be ex-husband wouldn't help pay for the divorce proceedings because his salary was at least three times the amount of mine. I was struggling financially just to pay for basic living expenses. He was the one who walked away from our marriage. "I love you; I just can't live with you" were his parting words. It hurt, but my armor strength increased that day.

I made several calls to find a suitable attorney to determine how much I needed to save for a divorce. I was able to locate a female attorney who appeared to be fair and affordable. She informed me that the divorce would be a relatively simple process because we had no children and no property. I informed my soon-to-be ex that I had retained an attorney, and that he would not be required to appear in court the day of the final proceedings. Now, I just had to save the money before anything further would proceed.

Prior to being hired at Casual Corner, I decided it was time to return to school and further my education. Early in my retail career, although I was a competent, fair, and respected manager, I was professionally unfulfilled. My desire to work in a university setting remained strong. I was ready to leave retail tasks behind. Those tasks included regular floor changes, conducting merchandise inventory, doing weekly markdowns, monitoring floor coverage for shoplifters, and assigning daily sales quotas.

As part of my pre-employment negotiation, I requested flexibility in my schedule to allow me to take classes without repercussion. I looked forward to both—a new job and the adventure being a college student once again. The silver lining that came with starting a new job and resuming my education simultaneously was that both were new opportunities for mental growth and professional enhancement. Both new ventures took my mind away from the discontent I felt with ending a damaged marriage that was long overdue to be dissolved. I longed for the day that I was trusting enough to let my emotions be available for a romantic relationship when the time arrived.

It was time to start using my brain for a higher level of critical thinking. After doing my research on programs that I wanted to pursue, Wayne State University was the best option. It was conveniently located; there were evening classes to accommodate my work schedule, and it was affordable—with the help of student loans. I was so excited to see the College Student Personnel (CSP) program offered in the Wayne State Graduate Catalog. I selected the master's program in CSP and I submitted my admissions application. Student Personnel work as a profession caught my attention while attending Bowling Green State University.

I was disappointed to learn that after the catalog was published, the CSP program had been discontinued. I received an offer of admission; however, it was to an alternate program in Counselor Education with a focus on Community and Agency Counseling. I was told that the counseling coursework was similar to that of the discontinued CSP program. I wasn't interested in becoming a counselor. I was informed that an internship in a college or university setting would be arranged near the conclusion of my coursework. I was also informed that the internship would provide me with sufficient experience to be a competitive candidate for most entry-level student affairs positions. I believed this was the right thing for me.

After being admitted to the program, I met with my advisor, Dr. Adam Huff and reviewed the plan for my educational program. The two courses that were recommended were Introduction to Counseling and Counseling Special Populations. I eagerly enrolled in two classes so I wouldn't overwhelm myself. I didn't want to potentially sabotage my educational or professional success. I had less than three weeks to adjust to my responsibilities of working with new staff at a new company, Casual Corner, before I began classes as a graduate student at Wayne State University in September 1985.

Early in my first semester, I began to struggle financially to the point where I needed to make a relatively quick decision about my living arrangements. I could no longer afford the studio apartment where I was living. I was trying to save money to cover attorney fees for the divorce. The financial pressure weighed me down. I didn't want it to affect my job or my performance in my classes. To make matters worse, I began having car problems. When it rains, it pours. I felt like I was being swept away in a massive flood with no end in sight. I needed a lifeboat or at the very least, a life jacket before I drowned.

Originally, when I moved to Detroit in 1984, Carole, mother of my soon-to-be ex-husband's best friend, Bobby, opened her home to me. I lived with her until I got settled into my job. At the time, she was recently divorced and living in the Boston-Edison Historic District in a grand home, less than a block away from what was known as the Berry Gordy Mansion. I lived in her home for about six months until I moved into an apartment located close to my job.

Fast forward to just over a year. I had to swallow my pride and ask Carole if I could move back into her home until I became financially stable. In hindsight, I probably moved out too soon the first time. Carole generously opened her home to me, once again, and I settled in the previous blue bedroom which was like an old familiar friend welcoming me home from a long journey.

I needed to focus my energy as a graduate student. The combination of work and graduate school were flowing along smoothly. I had made the right decision to return to school. I was energized by friendships with my new classmates. My work life was good, my living situation was on solid ground, and my classes were going well, or so I thought.

Accused of Cheating, Well Sort of...

From the beginning, both courses were interesting and manageable with my new job responsibilities. I was successful in completing all assignments. Being a graduate student, I embraced the learning process with a sense of pride and accomplishment. At the midway point of the semester, one of my classes included an assignment to interview a successful business owner or executive who we admired. This assignment was an opportunity for us to practice some of the basic counseling concepts during this informational interview process. The concepts we were learning included active listening, unconditional positive regard, empathy, and open questioning, just to name a few. The assignment included some basic questions to incorporate into our interview as prompts; otherwise, we were free to add questions that contributed to the interview.

I was in luck. Carole was a successful, Harvard educated, activist, entrepreneur and owner of many successful Burger King locations. There were many things that I admired about her business acumen and community achievements. She was the perfect person to interview. I told her about my assignment and asked if she would be willing to participate in an interview. She agreed and I scheduled an interview appointment with her, just as I would have with any other respected professional.

She was thrilled to be able to support my educational journey by being interviewed. With her permission, I recorded our interview so I could extract portions of our conversation for my assignment. I used a few of the prompting questions provided in the assignment. Because of her extensive professional history, I was able to practice my active listening skills, use empathy, with an occasional open-ended question for clarification. The assignment was not a direct transcript of our interview; however, she had so many extraordinary experiences, I quoted her several times and properly cited her direct quotes from the audio tape.

I was so excited following our interview. The finished product was masterful, in my humble opinion. I couldn't wait to turn it in because I felt like it was one of the best assignments I had ever completed, including my undergraduate work. I told Carole that she could read it after it was graded. As with all assignments in the Introduction to Counseling class, we were required to turn completed work in at the beginning of class. This was to demonstrate that assignments were completed on time as well as a method of taking attendance. There were absences of classmates on assignment due dates and it was noticed by most of my classmates, as well as the professor. I was eager to see how my assignment would be graded and looked forward to coming to class the following week.

One week passed and I returned to class with anticipation. Assignments were typically returned at the end of class, so I tried to be attentive and patient. Professor Adam Huff returned our assignments and I left the class, looking forward to reading any comments he offered about the amazing woman who had been the subject of my interview. I can remember being paralyzed in my tracks, standing in the hallway of the College of Education building, as I read the words written in a red, a barely legible scribble, on the upper right-hand corner of the front page. Although this is paraphrased, there are some things one never forgets. These words are seared in my soul forever.

"Did you write this or is it from a book?"

To this day, my nerves glow like red hot coals when I think of the insult to my integrity, the snub to my intellect, and the level of disrespect shown to Carole, the brilliant subject of my assignment. He casually wrote his callous remarks and thinly veiled accusations. Seeing his words, I knew that I had failed. Let me get this straight. Did he just ask me if I copied or plagiarized some or all of my assignments from a book? I had to look through my paper to see which part he indicated was copied. Where did he find evidence that what I had written was not properly cited? What other source had he found that included some or all of what I had written? There was no such indication. How dare he question my work without evidence! I was livid! As this played out in the hallway, I'm sure my classmates wondered what had me "stone statue" still in my tracks.

Oh! By the way, even after those awful words of accusation that tarnished this brilliant woman's story, that coward had the audacity to give me a "B" on the assignment. In graduate school, a "B" grade is on the edge of a failing grade. So, let me get this straight. You question the originality of my work. You provide no conflicting sources from which my original work was taken. You instill doubt in my ability to produce the quality of work that this assignment represents, but you don't have the courage to give me a "real" failing grade.

What you have demonstrated by the contradiction of your words, Professor Huff, is that rather than acknowledge the stellar work that this paper represents by giving me an "A," your ego is more comfortable putting those horrible words of accusation on this paper and assigning me a "B" grade. Does that "B" make you feel generous to this student from whom you expect only mediocre work? This was not about my ability. It was about his expectations. Dare I say it? His expectations of the ability of a black female student writing about a successful black businesswoman were confronted and his response played out on the front of my paper.

I realized that day that I had no empathy or unconditional positive regard for him. Thank God he wasn't a client. It would have been necessary to refer him to someone else and quickly. My level of respect for him disappeared that day. I decided that I would never take another class taught by this person. By the way, he was also my advisor, so that would change as well. Trust me.

Now, let me go home and share this graded assignment with Carole. It was late when I got home, but Carole was a night owl. I walked into the house. She was in the kitchen. I handed her the paper and let her read the comment. Carole is small in stature, about 5'5" tall. She's not someone who is easily intimidated or unnerved. When I say that she ignited like a match tossed into a gasoline can, that is an enormous understatement. She *blew up*! I already had my moments of extreme emotion with what I saw on the paper, so I gave her some time. As an academician, she also quickly looked through the pages to see evidence of his accusations. Seeing none, she proceeded to curse and express the things we could do to demonstrate our collective disdain for what he had said and done.

Carole was ready to ride out to Wayne State the next morning and offer Professor Huff a reality check of monumental proportions. She wanted to show him that she was an actual person—not a story from a book, and perhaps "throw" a few books at him. Okay, maybe I just took some creative liberty with my story, but she was ready to set him straight. I let her continue to verbally work through the emotions that I had already experienced. She eventually calmed down and we talked about what he had written and all that had transpired. In the back of my mind, I thought that maybe I returned to school too soon. Maybe this wasn't such a good idea. I wasn't ready to give up yet. I needed some answers.

I approached Professor Huff the following week, my paper with his remarks in hand. I asked him to clarify his written comment, and I asked about my grade. His response was weak and his justification was shaky. I'm paraphrasing his response, but he indicated that Carole's story sounded almost too good to be a real person. He explained that his comments were not meant to accuse me of copying someone else's work and that he was just impressed by the interview. He indicated that the grade would remain a "B."

For the remainder of the semester, I just did the work and counted the days to when the class would be over. My other class went well. The semester ended with a "B" in Introduction to Counseling and an "A" in Counseling Special Populations. Unbeknownst to Professor Huff, his cowardice act strengthened my armor, but those words that he scribbled on my assignment haunted me. I will not be contained by someone else's perceived limitations. The faint "limiting" words of that guidance counselor who suggested I become a factory worker or secretary echoed in my mind. I believe that she and Professor Huff were cut from the same judgmental, biased cloth.

From mid-November until Christmas Eve, retail is always extremely busy, so I was grateful when classes were over and the holidays passed. Work was going well. I was transferred to the Casual Corner store at Eastland Mall. One step closer to the promotion that I hoped was coming soon. By the time the "After Christmas" sales began to die down, I had registered to take classes in the winter semester. I was ready for 1985 to be over.

The new semester began and I attended classes for the first couple of weeks. My heart and mind were not in it, so I decided to withdraw from my classes. After doing some checking, Professor Huff was scheduled to teach a potential course on my plan. I was going to remain true to my word. I would never take another class under his direction. In addition, I had almost saved enough money to pay for my divorce and I looked forward to closing that chapter of my life as soon as possible.

The Good News, Really Good News

On the morning of Friday, March 7, 1986, I appeared at the circuit court in downtown Detroit. I met with my attorney, stood before the judge, responded to a few questions, and my divorce was final. Thank God! I was free of the emotional baggage that had weakened my spirit for too many years. I felt as if the weight of the world had been lifted from my shoulders. I did it. The financial cost paled in comparison to the gratitude I had for my emotional freedom and wellbeing.

I went to work that afternoon and shared the news of my divorce with my manager and the other assistant manager. I was giddy. Shortly after I arrived at work, I received a call from my district manager, Roni. She told me that she had some news to share with me. I remember exactly where I was standing behind the sales counter with my back to the store — which is an absolute no-no in retail, but my other coworkers were monitoring customers on the sales floor. I held my breath and listened very carefully. Roni proceeded to tell me that I was being promoted to manage my own store at the Northland Mall location of Casual Corner. My promotion would be effective in two weeks.

Nothing like this had ever happened to me. Two really great, life-changing events had just happened to me in the matter of hours. I was overjoyed. Finally, things were looking brighter professionally and personally. I looked forward to returning to Northland Mall. I had made friends with many of the merchants and sales associates there. I could see some of my former co-workers at Winkelman's. It was like a retail family reunion. Life was good.

I settled into my role as store manager and enjoyed several years managing some remarkable sales teams at both the Northland Mall and the Renaissance Center locations. I started dating some interesting and intriguing men. I was able to start saving money because of the raise that accompanied my promotion. I eventually moved into a small but affordable apartment near my work location.

I decided to return to my graduate program at Wayne State in the fall of 1987. My life had developed a rhythm, my confidence returned full steam, and I was determined to complete the educational journey that I started. I also made sure that I did not have any future classes taught by Professor Huff. I completed my master's degree in Community and Agency Counseling in June 1989. I knew at that point that my educational journey was not over, but I was prepared for whatever adventure was in store. After all, I had common sense and my trusty spirit of armor. Up to this point, neither had failed me yet.

Epilogue-The Story Continues

It was late July 1993. I was on a much-needed vacation in Gainesville, Florida. I had recently applied to the University of Toledo for the doctoral program in Higher Education Administration. I was eagerly awaiting a response. On

Friday, July 27, 1993, shortly after noon, I received a phone call from Dr. Jack Maynard, Associate Dean for the College of Education at the University of Toledo. In a pleasant voice with a slight southern drawl, he informed me that he was given the unfortunate task to call me and let me know that I was not admitted to the program. He was the messenger. He informed me that the committee that consisted of the department chair and others, had given names of applicants to individuals to contact and as associate dean, he was assigned the task of calling those who were not admitted.

I was devastated, but I remained composed as I asked him on what basis the admissions decision was made. He indicated that he had very little knowledge of the actual admission meetings or the notes related to the conversations. I asked him about the diversity of the incoming cohort and whether past experiences and success in previous graduate programs would have any bearing on admissions decisions. I informed him that I had completed a Graduate Record Examination (GRE) preparation course for the second time, prior to my second attempt taking the GRE. My performance was actually worse on the second GRE than it was during my first GRE attempt. I shared with him that, historically, I did not perform well on standardized tests, which typically did not accurately reflect my academic or intellectual capabilities, or my ability to succeed.

At that point I had nothing else to lose.

"What are the chances of my application being reconsidered?" I asked.

Our conversation continued, as he asked me a few more questions. He then instructed me to do the following: Document our conversation, indicating my history of unsatisfactory performance on standardized tests. He also suggested that I refer to my successful academic performance in my master's degree and my desire to be given an opportunity as a doctoral student at the University of Toledo. He asked me to fax my statement to him that afternoon so that he could present it to the admissions committee on Monday morning. By 4 p.m., I had completed my letter and faxed it to Dr. Maynard as requested. It was out of my hands.

My vacation was over, and the roller coaster of emotions I had experienced over the past week was overwhelming. When I arrived home the following Wednesday, August 1, I was unaware of what awaited me. As I plowed through the stack of mail that accumulated in my absence — bills, junk mail, catalogs — *wait! What is this?*

I came upon a letter with a return address from the University of Toledo, College of Education and Allied

Professions. I inhaled deeply and held my breath as I slowly opened the letter. I didn't know if I could take another rejection, not this soon. This is what I found upon slowly unfolding the single sheet of paper. (Yes! I saved it.)

Dear Ms. Clark:

This letter is in follow-up to your application for admissions to the doctoral program in higher education at the University of Toledo. Please be advised after reviewing your packet and the additional information that you furnished the department has decided favorably on your admissions application. The appropriate materials have been forwarded to the University's Graduate School and you should be receiving official notification in the near future. You have to know that the department had some serious reservations about your Graduate Record Exam Scores. However, we are willing to work with you and to give you an opportunity to demonstrate that you have the ability to succeed in this program...Best of luck in your studies. If you have any questions, please don't hesitate to contact me.

Sincerely yours,

Jack Maynard, Associate Dean.

I did it! Another battle won! However, I'm certain it's not the last battle that I will face where others try to displace their fears on me. Those years of building and strengthening my armor prepared me for many battles that lie ahead. I'm armored with hope and ready to go. Look out world! Dr. Farm Girl is just getting started.

"It's fear that makes an act courageous." ~Denise Hunter

About the Author

Dr. Mary K. Clark is a transformational leader who's empowered with her mother's quiet strength and her father's passion for social justice. Currently the assistant dean for Student Affairs at Wayne State University in the Eugene Applebaum College of Pharmacy and Health Sciences, Dr. Clark has nurtured, mentored and counseled thousands of college students to achieve professional success throughout the world. This national award recipient and caregiver advocate volunteers with AARP at the state and national level while maintaining her interests in genealogy, painting, and traveling.

Claire Aldin Publications is an award-winning, hybrid publisher. A proud member of the Independent Book Publishers Association (IBPA) with Better Business Bureau accreditation, our mission is to diversify publishing by providing education, tools and professional services to first-time authors from underrepresented backgrounds so their dynamic voices can be heard.

Special discounts are available on bulk quantity purchases of ten (10) or more by businesses, support groups, book clubs, ministries, associations or other special interest groups. For details, email **info@clairealdin.com** or call (248) 571-8227.

Want to know more?

Write to us at info@clairealdin.com

Or call 248-571-8227

www.clairealdin.com

Connect with us on social media:

@clairealdin

www.ingramcontent.com/pod-product-compliance
Lightning Source LLC
Chambersburg PA
CBHW030251030426
42336CB00009B/339